The Star of Bethlehem and Babylonian Astrology

Astronomy and Revelation 12 Reveal

What the Magi Saw

By Dag Kihlman

www.starofbethlehem.com

Dag Kihlman Publish
Boplatsgatan 1
461 57 Trollhättan
Sweden
www.starofbethlehem.com

ISBN: 978-91-639-2964-9
Copyright © 2017-06-11 by Dag Kihlman

All rights reserved. No part of this book may be reproduced or utilized in any form or by any means, electronic or mechanical, including photocopying, recording, or by any information storage and retrieval system, without permission in writing from the publisher.

Scripture quotes taken from:

The Bible (MEV), The Holy Bible, Modern English Version. Copyright © 2014 by Military Bible Association. Published and distributed by Charisma House, Florida. All rights reserved. http://modernenglishversion.com/

The Bible (NIV), The Holy Bible, New International Version, NIV Copyright © 1973, 1978, 1984, 2011 by Biblica, Inc. All rights reserved worldwide. http://www.biblica.com/bible/

The Bible (Berean), The Holy Bible, Berean Study Bible, BSB Copyright © 2016 by Bible Hub. All rights reserved worldwide. http://bereanbible.com/

Images reproduced with written permission from:

Figure 5 and Figure 20 © Trustees of the British Museum.
Figure 12 Photograph of door portal at St Trophime in Arles, France. © Keith Hall; used with permission obtained on 25th October 2016.
Figure 16 © Courtesy of the Oriental Institute of the University of Chicago.
Figure 19 © Forum Ancient Coins, www.forumancientcoins.com.

Other images are from Wikipedia or from the software program Starry Night. www.starrynight.com.

Contents

Preface	1
1 Basic astronomy	13
1.1 Why study astronomy?	13
1.2 Stars and planets	13
1.3 Constellations	13
1.4 Star signs	19
1.5 Retrograde motion	21
1.6 Conjunctions	23
1.7 Great conjunctions	24
1.8 The origin of the constellations	25
1.9 The names of the planets, their connection to gods and their role in divination	26
1.10 The names of the stars	27
2 The diviners in Babylon and their impact	29
2.1 What is divination and what is its relation to astrology?	29
2.2 Enuma Anu Enlil	32
2.3 What is a sign to be interpreted?	33
2.4 When signs were studied and what signs were studied	35
2.5 Babylonian divination for other countries	38
2.6 The development of astrology	40
2.7 The Babylonian priest Berossos and his emigration to Greece	41
2.8 The survival of Enuma Anu Enlil and the Mandaeans	42
2.9 Astrology and the Jews	44
2.10 Astrology and the Bible	47
2.11 Stars and angels in *The Book of Enoch* and in Qumran	50
3 What was a magus to Matthew and his readers?	53
3.1 Magi as officials in the Parthian Empire	53
3.1.1 The origin of the magi	53
3.1.2 The role of the magi in divination	54

 3.2 Chaldeans and the magi   56
  3.2.1 Magi as diviners, magicians and sorcerers   57
  3.2.2 Magi in the early Church   60
 3.3 Conclusion   62

4 Political history in the Middle East   63
 4.1 The rise of the Egyptian and Mesopotamian flood cultures   64
 4.2 The Akkadian Empire and the first Assyrian and Babylonian kingdoms   65
 4.3 The Neo-Assyrian and Neo-Babylonian Empires   66
 4.4 The Persian Empire   66
 4.5 The rise of the Greeks and Alexander the Great   67
 4.6 The Roman Empire   68
 4.7 The Parthian Empire   69
 4.8 Judah (Judea)   69

5 The cultural and religious development of Mesopotamia   72
 5.1 The status of Sumerian culture   72
 5.2 The Sumerian gods   73
 5.3 The Old Babylonian gods   74
 5.4 The Assyrian Gods   75
 5.5 The Neo- and Late Babylonian pantheon   75

6 The Babylonian gods and the signs of the gospels   76
 6.1 Ezekiel and the four-faced creatures   76
 6.2 Revelation and the four living creatures   78
 6.3 Irenaeus of Lyon and the four creatures   80

7 Astronomical events suggested to be the Star of Bethlehem   84
 7.1 The sceptical view   84
 7.2 Candidates for the Star of Bethlehem   87
  7.2.1 Comets and meteors   87
  7.2.2 Novae and supernovae   88
  7.2.3 Planets   88
  7.2.4 Stars   88

7.2.5 Constellations   89

7.3 The three main celestial events suggested to be the Star of Bethlehem   89

    7.3.1 Conjunction of Jupiter and Saturn in 7 BC   90
    7.3.2 Jupiter retrograding above Regulus in 3 BC and 2 BC   91
    7.3.3 Conjunction of Jupiter and Venus on 17th June 2 BC   93
    7.3.4 Combination of events in 3 BC and 2 BC   94
    7.3.5 The trip from Jerusalem to Bethlehem   96

7.4 Could a single planet be a sufficient sign?   100
7.5 Are we ready to draw a conclusion?   101
7.6 Is the sign about a New Alexander the Great?   102

    7.6.1 What we see in the stars   102
    7.6.2 The crowned woman clothed with the sun   103
    7.6.3 The pregnant woman   107
    7.6.4 The birth and the red crowned dragon/ serpent   109
    7.6.5 The fight between the archangel Michael and the dragon   111
    7.6.6 Conclusion about the woman and the fight   113
    7.6.7 The woman and her hiding place   114
    7.6.8 The woman and the baby snatcher   119
    7.6.9 Snatched to heaven   121
    7.6.10 The woman and the flood   122

7.7 Conclusion   122

8 Zoroastrianism   124

    8.1 The Zoroastrian sources   124
    8.2 Zoroaster   125
    8.3 The impact of Zoroaster   126

9 The Star of Bethlehem in a historical context   127

    9.1 Chapter outline   129
    9.2 Historical sources for dating the death of Herod/birth of Christ   130
    9.3 Ancient counting/dating methods   132

9.3.1 Regnal years	133
9.3.2 Consular years	134
9.3.3 Years since Rome was founded	135
9.3.4 Olympiads	135
9.3.5 How important were dates?	136
9.4 Josephus and his sources	136
9.4.1 How does Josephus count regnal years?	139
9.4.2 Calendar systems used by Josephus	140
9.5 The history of King Herod	145
9.5.1 Herod is appointed to be king in 40 BC	146
9.5.2 Herod becomes king in 37 BC	148
9.5.3 The Battle of Actium in 31 BC	153
9.5.4 Herod meets Augustus in 20 BC	154
9.5.5 The completion of Caesarea	155
9.5.6 The death of Herod	156
9.5.7 Herod's heirs	158
9.5.8 The case for 4 BC as the year of Herod's death	161
9.5.9 Conclusion	164
9.6 Quirinius and the tax registration	165
9.7 A critical view	167
9.8 Conclusion	167
10 The Gospel of John and the Book of Revelation	170
10.1 What do we know about John the Presbyter?	170
10.2 Was John the Presbyter a Babylonian? Was he a magus?	171
10.3 John the Evangelist	172
10.4 John the Evangelist and Ezekiel	173
10.5 Conclusion	174
11 Did Luke know about the Star of Bethlehem?	178
11.1 Did Luke know about the star?	178
11.2 Did Luke know about the magi?	179
11.3 What about the peace?	183
11.4 Conclusion	183

12 Consistency of the omens — 185
   12.1 Why compare omens? — 185
   12.2 Comparison of omens where the event is the same: how consistent are the predictions? — 185
   12.3 Consistency of the omens regarding Venus and Jupiter when both planets appear together — 188
   12.4 Conclusion — 191

13 Conclusion — 192
   13.1 What is the theory of this book? — 192
   13.2 What have we studied? — 193
   13.3 How should the Star of Bethlehem be examined? — 194
   13.4 Is the Bible a necessary reference in a valid theory? — 195
   13.5 What are the consequences for Christianity? — 196
   13.6 What are the consequences for Biblical science? — 198

Literature — 199
Registry — 203

Acknowledgments

I would like to thank my Ann-Britt for her patience with me during my work, and my sister Marina for reading this book when it was still in a poor state. I would also like to thank Fredrik Pommer Adler at www.ingridgopa.se for his help with photographs, websites and similar things. Finally, I would like to thank Natalie Cutting at www.youreyefordetail.co.uk for her valuable suggestions and improvement of the language.

Preface

This book will examine the story of the Star of Bethlehem, and the possibility that a group of people coming from the east visited Christ in Bethlehem. This group of people are called different things around the globe: wise men, magi and kings. In the Greek text, the word μάγυς (pronounced *magus*) is used. In this book, they will be called magi in the plural and magus in the singular. This is the word used by Matthew in Matt. 2. The word is not an invention by Matthew; it is a well-established fact that magi did exist in Babylonia and Persia. However, what has been unclear for two thousand years is where the biblical magi came from.

The story of the Star of Bethlehem is one of the best-known stories in the Bible, since it is repeated every Christmas. However, people differ in their attitudes to the story. Some consider it mere fiction; others believe that Christ was visited by some magi in Bethlehem, and that they were led to Bethlehem by the star. Some are open to the possibility that the story is true in some details, but not one hundred per cent fact. Others believe a true celestial event was known by the early Christians, who created a larger story out of this event.

In short, possible interpretations are numerous. The object of this book is to examine if the story could be true. If the result of the investigation is that the story could be true, this is not the same as saying that it must be true. We must distinguish between possibility and probability.

The purpose of this book is not to try to persuade the reader to change his or her opinion. However, the book aims to give the reader a basis for a rational conclusion. We shall examine different theories and examine the night skies. By gathering different theories and comparing them, the reader will have a more solid base for his or her own conclusions.

Of course, we must also examine the possibility that the story is fiction, or even fraud. In doing this, some readers might feel offended. However, an intellectual approach must allow all results, and readers must accept that some questions or examinations could be offensive to their existing beliefs.

An intellectual approach also involves being aware of any presumptions before the study: not only the presumptions of the author, but also of the reader. People feel strongly about religion. Some are strong believers and are willing to accept anything that supports their belief. Others are sceptics, and tend to avoid information that is contrary to their sceptical attitude. Neither approach is an open approach.

That Christ once lived on earth is accepted by most impartial people. So we have the following questions: could he have had any contact with the magi? If so, when did he have this contact? Or did his followers have contact with the magi, and invent the story later?

This book is a journey back in time to a place none of us can fully grasp. We will travel back to a time when diviners looked to the night sky to be informed about the future. They did not live in a Western society and they were neither Greek nor Roman; in short, we do not know very much about the people we are going to meet.

Traditionally, the Star of Bethlehem has been interpreted as a rare cosmic event, and this interpretation has been made by people who are accustomed to the traditions, history and beliefs of the Western world. A typical explanation of the Star of Bethlehem story is that someone finds what he or she believes to be a rare and strange real event, and within the blink of an eye, this event is identified as something the ancient diviners must have seen as being an omen about the birth of a king. If we want to find a sign, there will be many signs to choose from. However, the real question is whether there was any sign that would have been interpreted in a way that fits with the biblical description – not by us, but by the diviners living there at the time. Many explanations do not examine if these diviners would have interpreted the sign as the coming of a new king.

Because of this, there are many different and competing explanations. It need not be said that if one of them is true, others must be false. So is there any true explanation? Is the story of the Star of Bethlehem just fiction? How do we compare the different explanations? And how do we identify the explanations that are built on rock from those that are built on sand?

Many authors in the area falsely believe that divination by the magi reflects divination in Rome and Greece at the time:

> The extant writings of Greek, Roman, and Babylonian astrologers can give a very good impression of the astrological doctrines of the magi.[1]

This assumption is, as we shall see, completely unfounded. But since the idea is widespread, the theories about the Star of Bethlehem have never really been checked against how divination was actually performed in the East. Because of this, the present book is actually almost a pioneer work in this area.

In this study, a scientific explanation is built on arguments and proofs so that, in theory, everyone should be able to check the arguments and see if they stand up to critical examination. In reality, the situation is a bit more complex. In order to be able to examine the arguments, we need to have some basic knowledge about the area we are studying.

When it comes to the Star of Bethlehem, the area is very complex. Some explanations are built on the study of the Greek language used by Matthew in the gospel, so a critical examination must be able to

---

[1] Koch (2015), p. 60.

deal with this Greek text. We also need to have some knowledge about the stars in order to check if an event in the sky is ordinary, or seldom seen and exceptional. We need to know the basic assumptions used by the diviners at the time, as well as how they normally carried out their interpretations; we also need to decide where the diviners were from, and what their religion was.

In short, a complete study will cover many areas unknown to many of us.

As if this is not enough already, we will also have to know about the people and phenomena we are studying, and about ourselves. When we study a subject, we always do it from the point of view to which we are accustomed. We tend to believe that what we already "know" and believe is the correct information, and we are often cautious about new information that seems to contradict what we already "know". This is especially true when the information concerns our beliefs.

A person who strongly believes that Christ was visited by diviners in Bethlehem will probably continue to believe this even if we do not find any logical explanation for the story of the Star of Bethlehem. In the same way, a person with strong atheist beliefs will probably continue to see the story as fiction, even if we do find a good explanation. We tend to protect our basic beliefs.

A more scientific approach is to be open-minded and to try to find out what others believe and why, and then ask from a personal perspective, how good do we think their arguments are?

An open-minded approach also involves evaluating ourselves, and our own existing theories or beliefs. Little is known about the Star of Bethlehem, and many do not realise how little is said about it in the Bible. Some are convinced that there were three magi. Where does the Bible say that? Others are accustomed to thinking that the magi were kings, but the Bible never says that either.

Some believe that the magi left Jerusalem on camels and looked at the star in some sort of desert, seeking guidance as to where to go – but there is no desert between Jerusalem and Bethlehem. Such a belief is taken only from an ordinary Christmas card. The same is true of the belief that the star sent a beam of light down onto the face of the baby.

To make things worse, some believe that the magi saw the star "in the east", and others that they saw it "in the rising". The word ἀνατολή (anatolé), which Matthew used, actually means both, since the east is seen as the place of the rising. Some people argue strongly for the first translation, others for the second translation, and those who favour the second translation could choose see it either as the "rising of the star" or the "rising of the sun".

Others try to make a point of the fact that Matthew uses "east" both in the singular and the plural. He must have meant different things, people argue.[2] The case is a bit problematic for us to understand, since "east" is always singular to us. One way to have a better understanding of "east/easts" might be to try changing it to "eastern city/eastern cities":

> Wise men came from the eastern cities to Jerusalem, saying, "Where is He who was born King of the Jews? For we have seen His star in the eastern city and have come to worship Him.

If we change the text in this way, it becomes easy to imagine why Matthew used the plural for east in the general sense, and why he changed it to the singular when the magi talked about their own place. So the magi came from the "easts" (different eastern locations), but each of them came from just one "east" (their own eastern location).

---

[2] Koch (2015), pp. 81, 83.

People who argue over wording often forget to ask themselves whether Matthew really put so much thought into this word that a thorough analysis of it would reveal something? Matthew certainly had an intention when he wrote about the star, but he would not have been aware that some people would bend and twist every little word he used. To extrapolate a whole essay from his choice of words is merely an over-interpretation of what he has written. What matters is what people want to say, the message that they want to send. They choose the words to carry their message and expect people to hear the message, not to tear it to pieces in order to find hidden clues.

If Matthew wanted to tell us exactly what the magi saw and how they interpreted it, he would have written about it. He did not. To him, it was probably not important, or perhaps he did not know.

In the USA, a common theory is that what the magi saw is preserved in the Bible, in Revelation 12. It is a theory put forward by several different people. Central to this theory is the idea that Jupiter passed over a star called Regulus in such a way that it could have been interpreted as a crown. The name Regulus means "little king". Thus, Jupiter crowns the king, this theory says. Somehow, this is quickly seen as an omen about the birth of a new king. Larson is one advocate of such a theory.[3]

However, in Babylon at that time, the movement of Jupiter above Regulus was interpreted as meaning that the king would die, and that someone else would stand up and take the throne.[4] Thus, Larson's theory is built on a wish to find an explanation, rather than on historical facts.

---

[3] Larson (2017) is most often referred to as holding this theory.
[4] Rochberg (2010), p. 377.

However, it is too early to start evaluating different theories. In order to evaluate them we need to study how and where divination was performed, the diviners' religion and many other subjects.

A book dealing with so many different subjects will be challenging to read. It is much easier to read about one subject and increase our knowledge about that subject from chapter to chapter. In such a case, knowledge grows and deepens. In this book, such an approach would lead to the coverage of too many subjects at once. The chapters are thus more subject-oriented. The disadvantage of such an approach is that the book can be seen as avoiding the central subject: what was the Star of Bethlehem? Therefore, it is better to say what the conclusions of this book are now.

There are already several theories about the Star of Bethlehem, but most of them only have a poor foundation on historical facts and documents. Some can be proved to be impossible, if we evaluate them based on established facts.

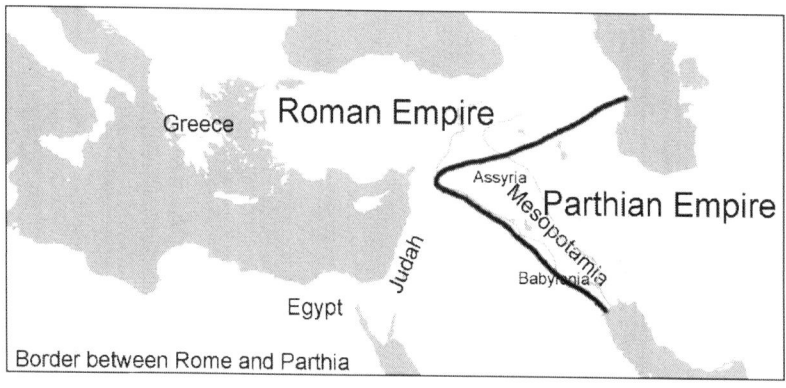

Figure 1. Map showing the border between Rome and Parthia

This book proposes a new theory: the diviners came from Babylon in Mesopotamia (see Figure 1) and used the ancient Mesopotamian divination manual, Enuma Anu Enlil. They looked at the night sky in September in 3 BC and in June in 2 BC. They concluded that the gods had decided that the king of Parthia should die. Parthia occupied Babylonia at that time, and they believed that the new king would be a kind of new Alexander the Great. Like Alexander the Great, the new king would come from a small state and overthrow a considerably larger state. This new Alexander the Great would have been or would be born somewhere in Syria, Lebanon, Israel or Jordan. In the sky, the angel/man, the lion, the bull and the eagle bore witness to this belief about the new king. Some readers will have noticed that the angel/man, the lion, the ox/bull and the eagle have been considered by the Church, since antiquity, as symbols for the evangelists.

The theory in this book is new and contrary to beliefs that people are accustomed to, and at first glance it seems far from the biblical story and impossible to prove. However, this theory is based on the Mesopotamian divination manual and real events in the sky, and is actually in full accordance with Revelation 12:

> A great sign appeared in heaven: a woman clothed with the sun, with the moon under her feet, and on her head a crown of twelve stars. 2 She was with child and cried out in labor and in pain to give birth. 3 Then another sign appeared in heaven: There was a great red dragon with seven heads and ten horns, and seven diadems on his heads. 4 His tail drew a third of the stars of heaven, and threw them to the earth. The dragon stood before the woman who was ready to give birth, to devour her Child as soon as He was born. 5 She gave birth to a male Child, "who was to rule all nations with an iron scepter." And her Child was caught up to God and to His throne. 6 The woman fled into the wilderness where she has a place prepared by God, that they may nourish her there for one thousand two hundred and sixty days.
>
> 7 Then war broke out in heaven. Michael and his angels fought against the dragon, and the dragon and his angels fought, 8 but they did not prevail, nor was there

a place for them in heaven any longer. 9 The great dragon was cast out, that ancient serpent called the Devil and Satan, who deceives the whole world. He was cast down to the earth, and his angels were cast down with him.

10 Then I heard a loud voice in heaven, saying:

"Now the salvation and the power and the kingdom of our God and the authority of His Christ have come, for the accuser of our brothers, who accused them before our God day and night, has been cast down. 11 They overcame him by the blood of the Lamb and by the word of their testimony, and they loved not their lives unto the death. 12 Therefore rejoice, O heavens, and you who dwell in them! Woe unto the inhabitants of the earth and the sea! For the devil has come down to you in great wrath, because he knows that his time is short."

13 When the dragon saw that he was cast down to the earth, he persecuted the woman who gave birth to the male Child. 14 The woman was given two wings of a great eagle, that she might fly into the wilderness to her place, where she is to be nourished for a time and times and half a time, from the presence of the serpent. 15 Then the serpent spewed water out of his mouth like a flood after the woman, that he might cause her to be carried away by the flood. 16 But the earth helped the woman. The earth opened its mouth and swallowed the flood which the dragon spewed out of his mouth. 17 Then the dragon was angry with the woman, and he went to wage war with the remnant of her offspring,

who keep the commandments of God and have the testimony of Jesus Christ.[5]

This book asserts that this theory best fits with what we know about divination, and furthermore does not contradict what the Bible says about the birth of Christ. The theory also fulfils the basic requirements for a valid explanation that a sceptic might have. For example, the sceptical astronomer Aaron Adair wants a theory that (a) is built on astronomical events; (b) explains why the diviners went to Jerusalem; c) explains how the star led them to Bethlehem; and d) explains how it could be that the star in question "stood still".[6] The theory in this book will satisfy all these demands.

Revelation 12 has been seen as astrology by some researchers. For instance, Tim Hegedus claims that Relevation 12 is connected to the constellations Virgin and Hydra.[7] He connects it to Greco/Roman astrology. This might be valid, since Virgo is a Greek constellation and the Babylonians called it The Furrow. On the other hand, if the magi did visit Bethlehem, what name would they use to explain what they had seen? Here we can only speculate.

Finally, it is good practice in a preface to say something about the structure and content of the book. We will start by looking at astronomy and divination generally, then we will look at the diviners in Babylon, or the magi specifically.

This book uses the word "divination" to mean the practice of reading the will of the gods in the skies, and reserves the word "astrology" for astrological practice as we commonly know it today in magazine horoscopes. When referring to the diviners in Mesopotamia, the word "magus/magi" will be used. It is also used for the diviners in Persia/Parthia. The reason for this is that astrology in the West was different from divination in the East. In

---

[5] The Bible (MEV), Revelation 12.
[6] Adair (2013), p 59.
[7] Hegedus (2007), p. 238

reality, there was no exact borderline, but the distinction is made to point out that Western astrology should not be automatically used when studying Eastern divination.

After studying basic astronomy and the main actors in divination, we will look at the political history and cultural development in the relevant area – mainly in Mesopotamia, but also in neighbouring countries. In connection to this, we should notice that the names of the area have changed over time. Mesopotamia roughly consists of Babylonia in the south and Assyria in the north. Babylonian culture is the best known, and so this book, like many others, tends to call the culture Babylonian, and the geographical area Mesopotamia.

After studying the relevant history and culture, we will be ready to look at different explanations for the story of the Star of Bethlehem. Although we will encounter Zoroastrianism during this part of the study, we will look deeper into this topic in a separate chapter.

Some readers will be aware that the dating of King Herod, Quirinius and the tax census are a bit problematic, and we will look into such questions in a separate chapter. For example, a sceptical reader will probably think that Herod died in 4 BC, in accordance with current scholarly opinion. This book agrees that according to the ancient historian Josephus, Herod died in early 4 BC. However, this book will produce strong evidence showing that Josephus tampered with his sources and reached 4 BC through his own calculations. His main source was the eyewitness Nicolaus of Damascus, an adviser to King Herod. Josephus states that Nicolaus only wrote while Herod was alive, and thus it might be that Josephus had no written source at all concerning Herod's death, which decreases the reliability of Josephus.

Next, we will look into the authorship of Revelation. Some Church fathers – that is, early influential Christian theologians – have questioned whether the author of Revelation and the author of the

Gospel According to John are the same person. What can be said about this, in the light of what we find in this study?

Matthew is the only evangelist who clearly mentions the star, though we will look into Luke as well – did he know about the Star of Bethlehem, and how does his story of the shepherds relate to it?

Since the book relies heavily on omens from Babylonia, a sceptical reader might wonder if the omens in this book were chosen because they fit the theory. Could there be other omens where the conditions in the night sky were the same, but the consequences differed? This is a good point, and in a separate chapter we will look deeper into the divination manual and see if it is consistent in its interpretations.

In the last chapter, a conclusion will be made on what this research has found. It is hoped that the reader will agree with this conclusion. If not, it is hoped that the reader at least feels that the facts gathered in this book have strengthened or improved his or her own conclusion.

1 Basic astronomy

1.1 Why study astronomy?

The majority of theories about the Star of Bethlehem are based on astronomical events. People claim that some events of this type are very rare, and thus would have made a great impact on the people who witnessed them. In order to evaluate such claims, we need to have some basic knowledge about how the stars and planets move.

Such knowledge is also crucial when we study omens. We need to learn some basic astronomical terminology in order to understand omens, since discussions of omens use such terminology.

1.2 Stars and planets

Everyone today knows the difference between a planet and a star, but for people in ancient times, this distinction was not as clear. The planets were seen as moving stars, for instance Venus, "the morning star". The word "planet" is actually a Greek word meaning *wanderer*.

1.3 Constellations

A constellation can mean two things. To the ancients, a constellation was a group of stars that together formed an object in the sky – normally an animal, a god or some other object. The stars were thought to be connected in a certain way, forming the image, and such an image is called an *asterism*.

Contrary to popular belief, there is no official list of asterisms. For example, anyone is free to draw Leo, the Lion, in any way they want. The reason for this is that the asterisms are of no real value to modern astronomy. To modern astronomers, a constellation is an area in the night sky, not a figure or a drawing. The sky is divided into small areas, with borders between them. To a modern astronomer, a star is in the Lion if it falls within the relevant borders.

The International Astronomical Union states that many different patterns exist, but none of them is the official pattern.[8]

Figure 2. Leo, the Lion, as an asterism and an illustration [9]

The lack of an officially established list of asterisms means that different types of software that produce images of the sky can display different asterisms. Most of the images in this book of the sky have been made with the software Starry Night.[10] Often, the images contain both an asterism and an artist's graphical illustration (see Figure 2). We can see that the artist has given the lion four feet, but the asterism does not have any feet at all! In fact, the Lion is actually drawn in several different ways. The reason is that the Lion is difficult to draw well.

Larson believes that the Lion has nine stars.[11] This is because he uses Starry Night and sees the image as illustrated above. In other

---

[8] See http://www.iau.org/public/themes/constellations.
[9] Image created with the help of the software Starry Night; see https://starrynight.com.
[10] See https://starrynight.com.
[11] Larson (2017).

software, the asterism has other stars, and other numbers of stars. For instance, it is common to include in the Lion a star that represents the end of the tail.

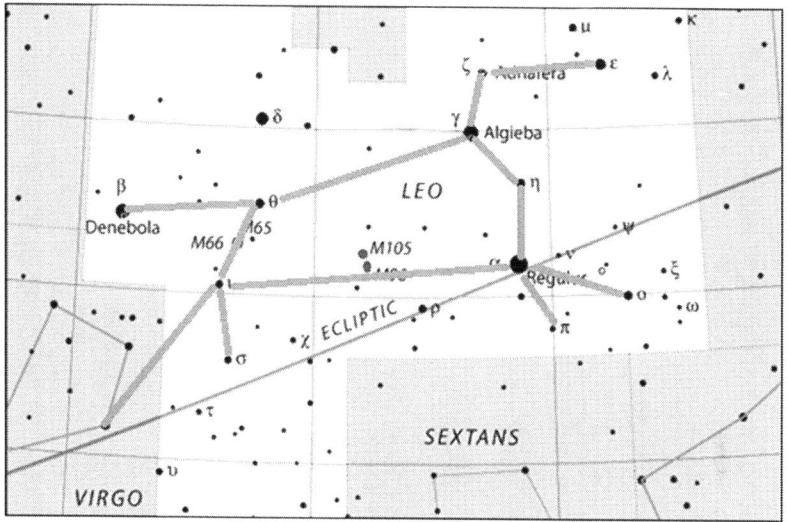

Figure 3. The Lion based on Mesopotamian star names

How could it be possible that the ancient astronomers made such a poor lion as the asterism in Figure 2? The answer is that they did not. Greek and Roman astronomers wanted to give the constellations clearer borders with more even widths. Because of this, some stars were moved from their original constellations. Originally, Leo probably looked more like Figure 3.

This asterism was made by the author of this book, and it is based on *star diaries* from Mesopotamia. Astronomers kept diaries of events in the night sky, and the times when these events occurred. Modern scholars have studied the diaries and deduced which star is which. It is possible to find this out, since modern mathematics and software can help us to see how the sky looked at different times. If the diary says that Mercury is at the star called "Right front foot of the Lion", we can identify the right front foot by looking at where Mercury was on the specified date.

The author of this book was unable to find a complete list of the stars of the Lion, neither in ancient sources nor in a list made by modern authors based on ancient sources. Therefore, the asterism is made with the help of many different sources. Thanks to their use of descriptive names for the stars, it is possible to identify several of the body parts of the Lion, and these sources thus partly help us to identify the asterism.

The parts known to us are:

1. Head of the Lion[12]
2. Regulus, the brightest star in the front of the Lion.
3. Right front foot of the Lion[13]
4. Foot in the middle of the Lion[14]
5. Rump of the Lion[15]
6. Tail of the Lion[16]
7. Rear foot of the Lion[17]

A foot in the middle of a lion sounds strange; maybe the expression "centre of the Lion" is better. In the asterism drawn above, it is assumed that the left back foot is intended. Other lists detail how many stars are found in the different parts of the Lion,[18] but these are actually lists of what can be found by looking in certain areas of the sky. Thus, there are two stars at the head, but only one star that is called the head. The stars in these lists were chosen to help draw vertical borders, and these were used for positioning purposes. In fact, these lists attempt to draw vertical borders so as to be used in the same way as modern astronomers use longitudes.

---

[12] Sachs and Hunger (1988), p. 7.
[13] White (2014), p. 379.
[14] White (2014), p. 379.
[15] Sachs and Hunger (1988), p. 7.
[16] White (2014), p. 380.
[17] Sachs and Hunger (1988), p. 8.
[18] Rochberg (2010), p. 292.

These lists are not thought to say anything about the asterism. In the case of the Lion, the star δ-leonis is included in the list even if θ-leonis is the rump and δ-leonis is far too high up to be included in the asterism. Thus, not all of the stars on these lists are suitable for inclusion. However, the lists do tell us that some stars are in certain places in the body of an asterism, so they give us information about the longitudes of the body parts of the Lion.

The suggested asterism of the Lion in Figure 3 was made based on the stars with descriptive names found in the sources. It uses eight of the nine strongest stars in the Lion. Some of the feet are represented by the fainter stars. The picture shows a lion with twelve stars. δ-leonis is the fourth strongest star in Leo, but since it is above the star known to be the rump of the Lion, it has been excluded in the asterism. Three feet are known in the sources. In order to make the Lion complete, one foot has been added.

There are very few drawings of the constellation from Babylonia and Egypt, but those we do have consistently represent the Lion with four feet and a tail going straight backwards. Thus, it seems very probable that the Lion originally had feet and a tail. Further, the back foot of the Lion is today a star belonging to the Virgin constellation. The right back foot and the tail, place the Lion firmly at the head of the Virgin, just as Revelation 12 says.

Roman and Greek astronomers moved the star that was originally the back foot of the Lion to the Virgin (seen on the left of Figure 3). Because of such alterations, some of the asterisms are distorted – if the lion loses one foot, the other feet are also likely to be lost in the process, since it would be strange to have a three-legged lion.

There are three main probable reasons that stars were moved in this way. By moving stars, the star signs had straighter borders between them, and the borders could be expressed as a degree of longitude; that is, a line going from the northern pole of the sky to the southern pole. Such lines and horizontal lines of latitude created a coordinates system that could be used to locate stars in longitude and latitude. The original constellations did not have sufficiently straight borders, and thus the longitudes were not as easy to describe and follow. Greek and Roman astronomers adapted the system from Babylonia by transforming the borders into straighter lines; they then categorised a large number of stars within each constellation.

Other reasons for the movement could be that ancient astronomers originally believed that stars always returned to the same longitude at an exact date every year – that is how the movements appeared to ancient astronomers. The Greek astronomer Hipparchus discovered that the constellations actually drift a tiny bit each year, and return to the same place in slightly less than a year. The stars seemed to "go before", and thus the phenomenon is called *precession*, a Latin word meaning "go before". This is the opposite of the better-known word, *recession*, meaning "going back". If a star passed the imagined border it might have been tempting to consider that star a part of the next star sign; since the Lion moved too fast, it might have lost its back foot to the Virgin.

The reason that we are paying such attention here to the original look of the Lion is that in Revelation 12, a woman is described as having a crown of twelve stars on her head. It has been suggested, and is also suggested in this book, that Revelation 12 describes events in the night sky in the years 3 BC and 2 BC, and that the woman is actually the Virgin star sign and the crown is the Lion.

As we saw in the preface, Tim Hegedus has also reached the conclusion that the woman is the Virgin. He believes that she represents the Queen of Heaven, since she is crowned. He connects her crown to the zodiac, and thus does not see it as a real crown in the sky.[19] The term used for the crown (of stars) is στέφανος ἀστέρων. Literally, this means "crown of stars" or "helmet of stars",

---

[19] Hegedus (2007), p. 234f

but a possible alternative translation is simply "headdress of stars".[20] Thus, Revelation 12:1 could be read as:

> A great sign appeared in heaven: a woman clothed with the sun, with the moon under her feet, and on her head a headdress of twelve stars.

1.4 Star signs

In horoscopes, star signs are used, and most of us know that the star signs are connected to constellations in the sky. The original meaning of star signs is that they are those twelve constellations in which the sun rises at different times of the year. In astrology, it is said that a certain star sign is *clothed* with the sun (see Figure 4 on page 20), and this makes it the presently active sign. In reality, the precession of the constellations has led to a mismatch between the dates used in astrology and the dates on which the constellations are actually clothed with the sun in our time. Today, a star sign is active depending on the dates established in Greek times, and different schools of astrology use different dates.

In Figure 4, we see the Virgin being lit up by the sun at sunrise on 13th September 3 BC. To make the image clearer, the daylight has been removed and the sun alone is seen on the left arm of the Virgin. In the figure, we can also see a line going through the sun and up to the rump of the Lion. This line is called the *ecliptic*, which is the name of the apparent path the sun takes around the sky in a year. Each day, the sun moves a bit further down the ecliptic. At an earlier date, the sun would also have been on the ecliptic, but higher up. One month earlier, the sun lit up the Lion, above the Virgin's head.

Since the sun moves along the ecliptic and since the star signs are the constellations along the path of the sun, the ecliptic goes through all the star signs. The planets, too, follow along this line,

---

[20] Liddell and Scott (1996), p. 650.

sometimes above and sometimes below the ecliptic. The same is true for the moon. To the Babylonians, this field of the sky, where the sun, the planets and the moon moved, was known as the *Path of the Moon*.

Figure 4. The Virgin at sunrise, 13th September 3 BC [21]

---

[21] Image created with help of the software Starry Night; see https://starrynight.com.

In the illustration, we cannot see the moon under the Virgin's feet, but the new moon is there, and the magi would have known that it was there. Another image from the same date, without the horizon and showing the moon, is seen in Figure 15 on page 106.

From an astronomical point of view, the text in Revelation describes the situation in September in 3 BC. However, Revelation 12 has removed all the names of planets and constellations. The reason is probably that star constellations and planets were connected to the heathen gods, and Jews and Christians were not supposed to use astrology.

To say that constellations and planets heralded the birth of Christ would have been open to the miscomprehension that the heathen gods heralded the birth of Christ, and that Christ thus belonged to the Greek and Roman religious system. It is thus possible that Revelation 12 wants to preserve the story, but hidden under a veil of parables.

Then again, critics will say that the moon will be at the Virgin's feet once a year when she is lit by the sun, and she will have the same crown as long as the earth continues to spin. This is perfectly true, and a sceptical reader might feel a bit uncomfortable with even the suggestion that Revelation 12 has anything to do with the night sky. Such scepticism and hesitation is a natural and sound reaction. In order to claim that Revelation 12 has anything to do with the diviners in Babylon, we must find more arguments. Reader scepticism is welcome, but patience is also a good and sound attitude. In order to see more connections between Revelation 12 and divination in Babylonia, we will have to study other things first.

1.5 Retrograde motion

Every day, the sun, the moon and the planets normally rise in the east and set in the west. But over the course of the year, the sun, the moon and the planets also move in this direction along the ecliptic. Therefore, if we look at Venus at a certain time of day, and then look at her at the same time the next day, we should expect her to have moved a bit further to the west.

However, the earth spins around the sun in the same direction as the other planets. Consequently, the earth will sometimes overtake the outer planets. In addition, half a year later the earth will be on the other side of the sun, in which case the earth will be moving in the opposite direction to the planets on the other side of the sun.

When the earth catches up with Jupiter, for example, it seems as if Jupiter moves more and more slowly. When the earth passes it, Jupiter will appear to move backwards, seen in relation to the background of the stars. This apparent movement backwards is called *retrograde motion*. The normal direction is called *prograde motion*. From the sun's point of view, all the planets move in the same direction. Retrograde motion is just an apparent movement in the opposite direction – we can see the same phenomenon in traffic as we overtake cars.

Jupiter will appear to move backwards for a while, but when the earth has moved on by a couple of months, this effect is reduced and Jupiter will appear to stop and change direction again. When the earth approaches the other side of the sun, Jupiter then appears to move very quickly in the right direction. At some point, when the earth is on the opposite side of the sun, we will not be able to see Jupiter, since the sunlight prevents us from doing so. To us, it might appear as if Jupiter at this stage is under the horizon, although it is actually behind the sun.

Since the earth overtakes Jupiter approximately once a year, Jupiter will appear to travel in both retrograde motion and prograde motion every year. When the planet switches direction, it will appear to stand still for a short time, and the place where a planet seems to make a stop is called a *stationary point*. There are two of these points, and they are called the *first stationary point* and the *second stationary point*: the first is the point at which a planet changes from prograde motion to retrograde motion, and the second is the point at which it changes from retrograde motion to prograde motion.

The inner planets – Venus, and especially Mercury – complete their revolution around the sun much quicker than the earth. As a result, the inner planets are often on the other side of the sun. Due to their faster speeds, these inner planets reach a stationary point more often.

The planets move approximately, but not exactly, on the same plane; that is, they cannot be said to be on a common completely flat disc. When a planet stops and changes direction, it will not follow exactly the same path as before. As a result, its path will look c-shaped when a planet changes direction, just as it would if we changed direction when driving a car. A full phase of going from prograde to retrograde motion and back to prograde motion will contain two stationary points – each of them will look c-shaped in the sky, and one of the c-shapes will be reversed. Both c-shaped turns together, with one reversed, will form an s-shaped path.

If two of the outer planets are close to each other, as seen from earth, they will perform the halt and the change of direction on approximately the same date. As a result, the planets will look a bit like they are dancing with each other.

Mars holds a special status in this respect, and the magi in Babylon actually called it the *Strange Star*. The reason is that Mars circles the sun in approximately two years, and thus moves much faster than Jupiter, which takes approximately twelve years to circle the sun. Because of this, the path of Mars is less influenced by the earth's movements, and the retrograde movements are less apparent.

1.6 Conjunctions

A conjunction is when two objects in the night sky come together. There is no clear rule as to how close two objects must be to qualify for the term "conjunction"; it is a matter of opinion. In the

Mesopotamian divination manual, the distance is measured in fingers, and a conjunction is described as a certain distance in fingers; that is, how many fingers we could put between the planets if we hold an arm straight out.

1.7 Great conjunctions

If Jupiter and Saturn are in the same area in the sky, as seen from earth, they will enter into retrograde or prograde motion at approximately the same time. They will seem to dance together, as explained above. Since Jupiter circles the sun in twelve years while Saturn takes thirty years, Jupiter and Saturn will "dance" once every 18–20 years. This number of years is not exact, since the planets do not have perfectly circular paths around the sun, and thus the speed varies a bit.

The meeting of Jupiter and Saturn is, of course, a conjunction. However, it should not be confused with the term *great conjunction*, which is a special conjunction occurring only once approximately every 800 years. This is like every other conjunction between Jupiter and Saturn, but for those who invented the term, a great conjunction marks the beginning of a new 800-year-long series of conjunctions, according to the following pattern:

For 200 years, the conjunctions of Jupiter and Saturn will appear in just three star signs. Then, for the next 200 years the conjunctions move to a new set of three star signs, and so forth. Each set of three star signs is called a *trine*. One of these trines consists of the Ram (Aries), the Lion (Leo) and the Archer (the Centaur/Sagittarius); this is called the Fiery Trine. When the circle of conjunctions moves back to Aries, Leo or Archer – that is, after a full 800 years – this return is called a great conjunction.[22] Some people call all conjunctions between Saturn and Jupiter great conjunctions, but

---

[22] Adair (2013), p. 62.

this is not the established definition, and it is not in accordance with the terminology used by ancient astronomers and diviners.

The 200-year-long pattern does not move sharply to a new set of constellations exactly every 200 years. The conjunctions can move to the new set of constellations, and then temporarily move back to the previous set, until the constellations have moved firmly to the new set. The great conjunction is the first conjunction in the Fiery Trine for 800 years, even if the next conjunction might fall in the previous trine.

1.8 The origin of the constellations

We do not know the origin of the constellations. It is probably the case that man wanted to see patterns in the sky, and has done so in different cultures around the globe for millennia. The constellations vary according to the culture being studied.

In around 1000 BC, the Babylonians had eighteen star signs; that is, eighteen constellations along the ecliptic. They reduced the number of star signs to twelve in about 500 BC. These star signs are pretty much the same as our twelve star signs today. The other constellations are also often inherited from Babylonia. The exception is the Virgin, which was called The Furrow. On the other hand the constellation is connected to fertility in both cultures.

We cannot tell when and how constellations were borrowed by the Greek culture, and we cannot even be certain that Greek culture did not influence the Babylonian view on constellations. However, it seems that the direction of the borrowing mainly went from Babylonia to the cultures nearby. This is not surprising, as Babylonian culture had a continual practice of writing and studying from the third millennium BC. A highly intellectual culture tends to spread its findings, thoughts and beliefs to neighbouring, less-developed cultures, as illiterate cultures are less likely to preserve their own traditions.

Constellations are not just hypothetical constructions. They can be used for navigational purposes. Therefore, one way the ideas could have reached neighbouring cultures was through navigation and foreign trade.

The star signs are the best-known constellations because the planets and the moon go through them. Astronomers recorded how the planets and the moon moved, and related their observations to the constellations in which the planet or moon was located. Consequently, we have many texts about the constellations along the ecliptic.

The other constellations are less well known to us. We have more difficulties understanding their names and asterisms. In some parts of the sky, we do not even know whether the Babylonians had asterisms.

It is not easy to draw a map of the night sky, and we have very few illustrations of the sky. Scholars have studied the constellations in Babylonia and found them to be similar to the constellations used in Greece and Rome. In this study, we do not need to know exactly what all the constellations looked like. The main constellations used in divination are the star signs, and we have a very good idea of how they looked to the Babylonians.

1.9 The names of the planets, their connection to gods and their role in divination

The English names of the planets are the same as the names of Roman gods. The idea to connect the planets to the gods was probably imported to Greece from Mesopotamia. The oldest known names for planets in Greece are not the same as the names we find in Greco-Roman times.

In Babylonia, the planets were connected to gods, but were not always named after them. The Babylonian pattern is that the highest god is represented by the planet Jupiter. Mars and Saturn are male war gods. Venus is a female goddess of fertility and Mercury is a male god. This pattern is repeated in Greece and Rome, although Saturn is not seen as a war god, and Mars is seen as a good war god; in contrast, in Mesopotamia Mars was seen as an evil war god.

Thus, the names of the planets ultimately go back to the Babylonian pattern of connections between gods and planets. The roles of the gods – with Jupiter as the highest god, Mars as a war god and Venus as a fertility goddess – are also very similar.

When people try to understand the nature of the Star of Bethlehem, they tend to look at the planets in the Greek and Roman way, and this seems to be a good approach because of the similarities between the Greco-Roman and the Babylonian system. However, the omen system in Babylonia is far more complicated than this.

An extreme conjunction is when two planets come so close that they appear to merge into one single object. Some people think that the merging of Venus and Jupiter into one single star on 17th June 2 BC was interpreted as the birth of a prince. The logic is that Jupiter stands for kingship, and Venus for fertility and reproduction. A merging of the king planet and the fertility goddess must, thus, be seen as the production of a child – a new king – or so some claim.[23]

However, the Babylonian interpretation for this event was that the king of Akkad would die. To use the Western, ultimately Greco-Roman, understanding of things is thus completely misleading.

1.10 The names of the stars

Some of the stars have names that ultimately come from the Babylonians, but are known in their translation to Latin. In our study, the star Regulus is important. Its name means *little king* in

---

[23] Larson (2017).

Latin. To the Babylonians, it was called Lugal, the King.[24] Another name for it is Cor Leonis.

It is beyond the scope of this book to examine other stars, since Regulus is the only one of interest here. It is sufficient to say that the Greek and Roman world borrowed heavily from Mesopotamian culture, and things said to be invented in Greece or Rome were often just borrowed from Mesopotamia. However, there was little interest in recording the culture and history of Mesopotamia in Greece or Rome, so at present we know very little about it. But numerous cuneiform tablets remain to be translated, and we can be confident that many surprising finds will be made in the future.

---

[24] Sachs and Hunger (1988), p. 7.

2 The diviners in Babylon and their impact

2.1 What is divination and what is its relation to astrology?

Divination in Mesopotamia has been practised since at least the second millennium BC. The practice of divination is based on the sun, the stars, the constellations and the planets, but it was studied in a completely different way than in Greek and Roman astrology.

Astrology is primarily focused on the moment of a person's birth. Which constellation was active, and how did the moon and the planets stand in relation to each other at that point? Based on such questions, a horoscope is worked out. The word "horoscope" consists of two words: horo, meaning "time"; and scope, meaning "what is seen". Thus, a horoscope is what is seen at a given time.

The position of the planets at birth is called a *natal chart*, and this is the scope of what can be seen at birth. Based on the natal chart, a horoscope for life can be written. It gives details about what a person is like, what his or her strengths and weaknesses are, what he or she might become and what he or she should avoid. Astrology is not the same as predetermination. Two people born at the same time on the same day will get the same predictions. However, the consequences of the natal chart do not decide the actual outcome; what a person does with the strengths and weaknesses given to him or her at birth also matters.

Since astrology is based on an evaluation of strengths and weaknesses, two astrologers will not produce the same prediction. There will be some similarities, but the relations between the stars and planets are not evaluated in a strict mathematical fashion. It is a matter of judgment and personal opinion.

Divination in Mesopotamia was quite different from astrology as we know it today. Firstly, it had nothing to do with the situation at birth; secondly, it was not open to everyone. At that point in time, the main user of astrology was the highest king in Mesopotamia.

Figure 5. A tablet from Mul Apin [25]

We cannot say to what extent the diviners might have used divination personally. However, divination concerned the state, the

---

[25] © Trustees of the British Museum.

welfare of the king, war, harvests and diseases and other catastrophes. Some part of divination also concerned the welfare of other countries. The king would naturally have an interest in learning what would happen to his allies and enemies.

Since the king was the main recipient of these predictions, it would have been very strange – indeed, possibly dangerous – if the diviners had differed greatly in their interpretations. It also seems that divination was an occupation that was inherited, a practice passed on from father to son. Due to these factors, a group unknown to us developed a manual for divination – Enuma Anu Enlil. As we will see below, it leaves little room for alternative interpretations when looking at singular events in the sky.

It is unfortunately difficult to obtain a photograph of one of the tablets in the manual. However, a related text is Mul Apin, which describes which times of year principal stars rise over the horizon at sunrise. This series of tablets is crucial for finding out the names of different stars. One of these tablets is presented in Figure 5, although this is actually a negative in clay. The Babylonians could reproduce tablets by first writing one tablet, then pushing clay into the signs and making a reversed tablet. This could in turn could be used as a negative to reproduce copies of the original text. Researchers have been able to reconstruct some texts by observing that small pieces are made from the same negative. Small fragments of a larger text can be pieced together, and the reconstructed text is longer than each fragment.

A critical reader might object to what has been written here about Greek astrologers, and say that they were not only interested in natal charts, but also looked at divination more generally. This is true. The Greek and Roman astrologers were interested in Babylonian divination, but on the whole, they performed astrology based on natal charts. The main point here is that Babylonian divination had nothing to do with natal charts.

2.2 Enuma Anu Enlil

Ancient Mesopotamian documents are named after their first words. The divination manual begins with *Enuma Anu Enlil* …, which means *When Anu [and] Enlil* ….[26] The manual is very straightforward and simple to use. A condition is described, and a consequence predicted:

> If Jupiter passes at the head of Venus, Akkad will be conquered with a strong weapon.[27]

The text always uses the name "Akkad" for Mesopotamia, and the king was referred to as "the king of Akkad". This was an archaic title going back to the Akkadian Empire (see Chapter 4.2). The Babylonians had a continuous culture and were aware of the history of the area. By using these terms, the omens seem to be very archaic, and the authors probably consciously used this title to make the omens look ancient, something like a thousand years older than they probably were.

We do not know the exact age of the manual. It consists of sixty-eight or seventy tablets, and the number of omens is estimated to be anything up to around seven thousand. The omens are based on the movements of the planets among the stars, the appearance of the moon and lunar eclipses, the appearance of the sun and solar eclipses, and even earthquakes and thunder.[28]

The series is not complete, and different versions – perhaps five of them – exist. The oldest copies are from the seventh century BC[29] and the latest dateable copy is from the early second millennium BC. It was exported to India in the third century BC or earlier.

---

[26] Rochberg (2004), p. 70.
[27] Reiner (2005), pp. 41, 47, 51. The rule is found on several tablets but there are some difficulties reading a complete rule on a single tablet. However, the quotation is based on several tablets and the correct reading is clear.
[28] Rochberg (2004), p. 67.
[29] Rochberg (2004), p. 66.

It seems that divination began in the early second millennium BC, and it became very popular in the first half of the first millennium BC, spreading to neighbouring cultures at about the same time. The forerunners of Enuma Anu Enlil are dated to about 1200 BC, but the mature form of the series is found in Assyria in about 700 BC.[30]

In the second millennium BC, we find texts that mention the "scribes of (the celestial omen series) Anuma Anu Enlil".[31] These scribes were employed at the Marduk temple Esagila in the city of Babylon. Evidence suggests that the old traditions were preserved in Babylon through to the first century AD.[32]

The best-preserved versions of the above are from the library of king Ashurbanipal of Assyria. Among the most important finds in this library is a table of contents, which details the number of tablets and what different parts of the text are dealt with.[33]

The omens in the text are surprisingly free of references to the gods, although some gods are mentioned occasionally. In this way, the manual could have been used in Assyria as well as in Babylonia and some neighbouring areas, without being offensive to the local religion. Babylonia and Assyria shared many gods, but the role and status of the gods differed depending on time and place. Thus, the omen series was not greatly affected by changes in religion.

2.3 What is a sign to be interpreted?

In Enuma Anu Enlil there are several types of omens, as mentioned above. In this book, the interest is only in omens concerning the moon, planets and stars, and to some extent, the sun.

---

[30] Rochberg (1998), pp. ix–x.
[31] Rochberg (1998), p. 5.
[32] Rochberg (1998), p. 12.
[33] van der Waerden and Huber (1974), p. 49.

A star and a planet were the same thing to the diviners in Mesopotamia. A planet is simply a star that is wandering – just as it was to the Greeks, as explained earlier.

Planets were connected to gods, and Jupiter was seen as the highest god, Marduk. Saturn was Ninurta, Mars was Nergal, Mercury was Nabu and Venus was Ishtar. The gods could also be connected to a star constellation. Marduk was connected to Taurus (the Bull), and Nergal to Leo (the Lion). Ninhursag was connected to Virgo (the Virgin).

The word for star, MUL[34], is the same as the word for planet, which is not surprising since planets were seen as stars. However, MUL could also be used for a whole constellation, because its basic meaning is "sign"; the same word is actually used for signs in cuneiform writing.[35] So if the magi really came from Mesopotamia and told Herod that they had seen the new king's star, we must be open to the idea that this might mean they had seen a planet. It could also have meant that they had seen his sign more generally.

That the star is said to have went before them from Jerusalem to Bethlehem points to them having seen a single planet. In reality, the sign was not the planet itself, but rather what the planet actually did. Therefore, if the magi came from Mesopotamia and said that they saw the new king's star, they would have meant that they saw a planet doing something. This event was the sign that foretold what the newborn would achieve in life. The sight of a planet or star it itself would not have told them anything.

---

[34] Astrologists normally use capitals in translations of cuneiform text. This practice is followed here.
[35] Rochberg (2004), p. 2.

2.4 When signs were studied and what signs were studied

The Babylonians had the same concept of months as Jews have today. The month begins on the evening of a new moon. To follow the moon was thus very important, and to do so across the kingdom would ensure that the same calendar could be used everywhere. If the new moon was not seen in the evening for some reason, it would probably be seen later in the night or the next evening. The month could in such cases start one day later than expected.

In Babylonia, the system of months was regulated into a nineteen-year pattern, which was repeated. The same system is used today by the Jewish calendar. However, this system was not used by the Jews in the first century AD, so in reality the first day would fall on the stipulated day among the Babylonians, while Jews still looked to the night sky to learn when the month started.

The evening watch was thus important, but even more important was the morning watch. The magi wanted to see how the moon looked at the daybreak of the new month. If the horns of the moon – that is, the ends of the crescent – were visible and clear, it was a good sign for the new month. If clouds darkened the horns, or if atmospheric dust made the moon red, it was seen as a bad omen. Enuma Anu Enlil also mentions a middle watch, so three watches each night are assumed in the manual. Whether these watches were kept, we cannot tell.[36] Of course, this is a matter of time and money available for the study, and it probably varied through the centuries.

For centuries diviners studied the night sky, and researchers have found a long series of astronomical diaries made in Mesopotamia. Such diaries have been dated as coming from several different centuries in the first millennium BC. The earliest recorded year is 651 BC, and the latest known diary is from 60 BC. The diaries

---

[36] Reiner (2005), p. 125.

contain the positions of planets, and they were probably used in divination to be able to forecast the future more accurately than by day-to-day observation. Many planets have regularities in their patterns, so by knowing the paths of the planets in the past, the diviners were able to forecast how they would move in the future.[37]

The diaries contained information about:

- The moon
- Planets
- Solstices and equinoxes, Sirius phenomena
- Meteors, comets, etc.
- The weather
- The prices of commodities
- The river level
- Historical events[38]

Concerning the planets, information was recorded as to when planets passed a so-called *normal star* when this became visible in the sky, and when it disappeared under the horizon. Information was also recorded about when a planet *stood* – that is, when it appeared to stop before changing direction (the stationary point, as discussed in Chapter 1.5).[39]

The concept of a normal star is not the opposite of an abnormal or strange star. The word is a heritage of the language of one of the first people to translate the diaries – the German scholar Epping. He used the word "normalsterne" as a translation of an Akkadian word meaning "stars of counting, predictable stars". A normal star is a star on or close to the ecliptic, which is the apparent path of the sun, or the path drawn on the sky if one follows the position where the sun rises for a whole year (see Chapter 1.4).

---

[37] Sachs and Hunger (1988), pp. 4, 12.
[38] Sachs and Hunger (1988), p. 4.
[39] Sachs and Hunger (1988), pp. 6, 12.

Some thirty-two stars along the ecliptic were chosen and used as a system of reference points. The position of stars was recorded as so-and-so-many fingers or cubits to the left or right of a normal star. A cubit was twenty-four fingers. Today, we use degrees for the same purpose.[40]

The last diary found is from the year 60 BC, as mentioned above. This does not mean that the diaries stopped being kept after this point. We know that the magi in Babylonia kept working into the second century AD (see Chapter 2.2). We have no proof that diaries were kept, but this was such an important task in research and divination that we have no reason to doubt that they were, even though we have not found them. However, a shorter almanac has been found concerning the months of August and September in 7 BC:

> Month Ulūlu, [beginning on the] 30th [of the preceding month]: Jupiter and Saturn are in Pisces, Venus in Libra, Mars in Scorpio. On the 12th: Venus reaches Scorpio. On the 14th: full moon. On the 21st: Jupiter rises at the [beginning of the] night. On the 21st: Mercury appears at sunset; missing. On the 21st: Saturn rises at [the beginning of] the night. On the 28th: Mars reaches Sagittarius. On the 28th: [last moon]rise [before sunrise].[41]

Thus, we have no reason at all to doubt that the magi were examining the skies at the time of Christ's birth, and we have no reason to doubt that they were still observing the skies in the evening as well as in the morning.

When discussing written material from Mesopotamia, we shall keep in mind that the use of clay tablets was rapidly decreasing at this time, and the scribes had turned instead to using perishable

---

[40] Sachs and Hunger (1988), pp. 6, 10.
[41] Koch (2015), p. 141.

materials, such as papyrus. That the amount of evidence from this period declines is thus not proof that the practice of divination was declining.

2.5 Babylonian divination for other countries

Some of the rules in the divination manual clearly point to other countries:

> If Jupiter enters inside the Moon [i.e. is eclipsed by the Moon]: there will be famine in Amurru, the king of Elam will perish by weapons, Subartu ... will revolt against his lord.[42]

Amurru is the same as the word Amorite used in the Bible. Amorites had immigrated to Mesopotamia, but in Enuma Anu Enlil the Amorite area is the same as the Levant – that is, west Syria, Lebanon, Israel and Jordan.

The names used suggest that Enuma Anu Enlil was written in the latter half of the second millennium BC, but the names could also have been chosen consciously to make the text appear older. The use of the name Akkad is certainly done to make the text seem old.

Other countries could be included in divination in two other ways: firstly, some signs could involve some other unnamed country. If such a sign appeared, it could be assumed that the sign concerned a country in the direction of the sign. Secondly, a sign could be connected to a country due to the direction of the wind when the sign was observed.[43]

---

[42] Reiner (2005), p. 71.
[43] Koch-Westenholz (1995), p. 106.

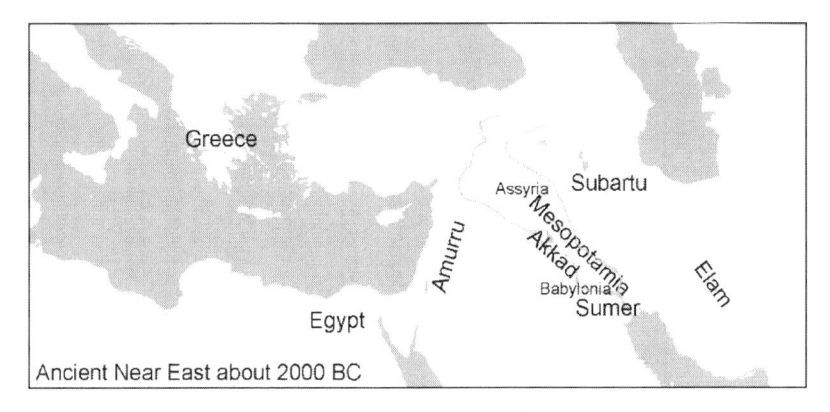

Figure 6. Compass directions in Enuma Anu Enlil

Some countries were also used as general directions. Amurru is to the west, Subartu to the north-east and Elam to the south[44] (see Figure 6). Subartu was mentioned in the sources occasionally from the third to the first millennium BC.

Primarily, divination aimed to tell the king of Akkad what the gods were planning, and signs normally concerned Mesopotamia. In Greco-Roman astrology, some constellations were connected to certain geographical areas. To see a sign in a certain constellation would then suggest that the sign concerned that geographical area. This was definitely not the case with Babylonian divination.

If Enuma Anu Enlil was what directed the magi to Jerusalem, we should look for signs about Amurru. If the sign happened in the west, it could strengthen the interpretation that Amurru was involved, if Amurru was already mentioned in the divination manual. To assume that a sign concerns the west because it was seen in the west is a mistake that has been made by others, such as Larson.[45] However, we shall see that the sign Larson discusses does concern Amurru, according to the divination manual (see Chapter 7.3.3). Thus, the direction of the sign strengthens the interpretation.

---

[44] Rochberg (2010), p. 46.
[45] Larson (2017).

In the Preface, the main theory of this book was presented: that the magi thought that the king of Parthia was to be replaced by a newborn king from Lebanon, Syria or Palestine. Several omens on two different dates support this theory. One of these signs was the sign mentioned above, which told the magi that a new king was to come from Amurru. Larson has picked the right sign, but his interpretation is not the same as the magi's interpretation.

2.6 The development of astrology

In this book, divination is considered to be the practice of seeing a condition in the night sky and making a clear prediction based on that. Such divination is at the core of Enuma Anu Enlil's astronomical divination. The same pattern was used to interpret other omens, such as earthquakes. Things happened, and the manual predicted the consequences.

In contrast, astrology is considered in this book to describe the study of the stars, which we find in magazines even today. Another way of putting it is that the word "astrology" is used for Greco-Roman divination. We have seen that according to such astrology, the planets have a certain influence on people depending on when they were born.

In reality, this distinction between Greco-Roman and Babylonian divination is more theoretical than real. Astrologers in Greece and Rome knew and practised both forms of reading the night sky. The methods are complementary, but natal charts were not originally a Babylonian practice.

These two ideas have since merged in astrology: the idea that the birthdate has influence and the idea that the stars tell the fates. To the diviners in Babylon this was an unknown idea, but of course, they would meet the idea at the time of Alexander the Great's conquest of Mesopotamia. After this time, we find natal charts in Mesopotamia, suggesting that these practices had spread there. The earliest obvious natal chart is from 325 BC, which is a couple of years after Alexander the Great's conquest.[46] An older chart may have been found from 410 BC, but in this case, only the position of the stars is preserved. However, it is likely that it is a horoscope.[47]

Astrology seems to have developed within Greek culture, perhaps in Egypt. From Babylonia, astrology inherited the idea of the planets as agents telling the future. Some influences also seem to have come from Egypt, but the roots of astrology are little known.[48] From a practical point of view, the idea of a natal chart made it possible for the diviners to gain a larger market for their services.

2.7 The Babylonian priest Berossos and his emigration to Greece

In the beginning of the third century BC, Berossos, a priest and magus belonging to the god Marduk's temple in Babylon, either emigrated or was brought as a prisoner to the Greek island of Kos.[49] He presented Babylonian culture to the Greeks (see Chapter 5.1), and according to the Roman writer Vitruvius, also established an astrological school in Kos:

> The talent, the ingenuity, and reputation of those who come from the country of the Chaldeans [i.e. the Babylonians], is manifest from the discoveries they have left us in writing. Berosus was the first of them. He settled in the island and state of Cos [latin spelling for Kos], and there established a school. Afterwards came Antipater and Achinapolus, which latter not only gave rules for predicting a man's fate by a knowledge of the time of his birth, but even by that of the moment wherein he was conceived.[50]

---

[46] Campion (2008), p 176.
[47] Rochberg (2010), p. 192.
[48] Campion, (2008), pp.104–108, 219.
[49] von Stuckrad (2015), p. 390.
[50] Vitruvius Pollio (first century BC or AD), Book IX, Chapter 6:2.

No one questions that Berossos was Chaldean, but some have questioned whether Berossos really came directly from Mesopotamia or whether he came via Egypt. We do not know exactly where astrology as we know it emerged, but it probably grew out of a mixture of different traditions. We also cannot tell for sure how Berossos contributed to this development. The school he is supposed to have established is only known from Vitruvius, who was born about two hundred years after the death of Berossos, and the school could be something Vitruvius invented because he thought it plausible that an early, well-known Chaldean had influenced later Chaldeans.

2.8 The survival of Enuma Anu Enlil and the Mandaeans

Much of the speculation about the Star of Bethlehem assumes that the magi used Roman or Greek astrology to interpret the sky. This is of course possible, but we also know that Enuma Anu Enlil survived into the first millennium AD, and that the basic ideas were transmitted to the Mandaeans – that is, the followers of Mandaeism.

The Mandaeans are an ethno-religious group indigenous to the alluvial plain of southern Mesopotamia. They have a book called *Sfar Malwasia* (alternatively *Asfar Malwasia*), which contains omens that are clearly preserved from Enuma Anu Enlil. The origin of this book is not clear, nor when or how the omens in it appeared, but evidence suggests it was written several centuries after the birth of Christ. The oldest copies are from the nineteenth century AD, but the content points to it having been written some centuries after the birth of Christ.[51]

The *Sfar Malwasia* is sufficient proof to conclude that Enuma Anu Enlil was available in some form when Christ was born. The fact that we do not have any copies of Enuma Anu Enlil from these

---

[51] Rochberg (2010), pp. 223–235.

dates probably reflects the fact that the magi already had the text on papyrus.

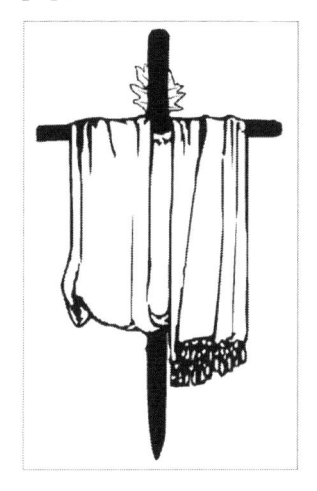

Figure 7. The Mandaean cross [52]

The Mandaeans are of interest to the history of Christianity in other aspects. They are, contrary to their own claims, thought to be descendants of immigrants from southern Jordan or Israel. Their ancient language has great similarities with the language used in the Babylonian Talmud, and John the Baptist is also one of their prophets. They consider Christ's mother, Mary, to be Mandaean, but reject Christ. Their symbol is a version of the cross (see Figure 7).

Some who do not believe in Christ, are quick to find the "true" roots of Christianity in obscure documents and religious sects. To such people, the Mandaeans are an interesting subject. However, the content of Mandaeism suggests that it contains roots from several other religious beliefs and practices from the third century AD, such as Manichaeism, for instance. Thus, Mandaeism

---

[52] Mandaen Cross, © Original from https://en.wikipedia.org/wiki/Mandaeism#/media/File:Darfash_-_Mandaean_cross.png by user Dragovit on Wikipedia.com. Used under licence; see https://creativecommons.org/licenses/by-sa/3.0.

arrives too late to explain the rise of Christianity, and the cross is likely to be something borrowed from the Christians, and not the other way around.

2.9 Astrology and the Jews

The Jews encountered divination in several ways. In the Bible, divination is explicitly forbidden, although from the text, we understand that divination was used by people in neighbouring countries.

> 9 When you enter into the land which the Lord your God gives you, you must not learn to practice the abominations of those nations. 10 There must not be found among you anyone who makes his son or his daughter pass through the fire, or who uses divination, or uses witchcraft, or an interpreter of omens, or a sorcerer, 11 or one who casts spells, or a spiritualist, or an occultist, or a necromancer. 12 For all that do these things are an abomination to the Lord, and because of these abominations the Lord your God will drive them out from before you. 13 You must be blameless before the Lord your God.[53]

Among the persons practising divination, Balaam stands out. He is mentioned in Numbers 24:17, where he says:

> 17 I will see him, but not now; I will behold him, but not near; a star will come out of Jacob, and a scepter will rise out of Israel, and will crush the borderlands of Moab, and destroy all the children of Sheth. 18 Edom will be a possession, and Seir, a possession of its enemies, while Israel does valiantly. 19 One out of Jacob shall have dominion, and destroy the survivors of the city.

---

[53] The Bible (MEV), Deuteronomy 18:9–13.

Jewish kings during the second century BC started to see themselves as the fulfilment of this prophecy, and Jewish kings and leaders continued to do so down to the Bar Kokhba revolt in the second century AD. The leader of this last revolt was Bar Kokhba, whose name meant "son of the star".[54] The early Christians also connected Christ to Balaam, and the Star of Bethlehem was seen as Balaam's star (see Chapter 3.2.2).

The Jewish authors Josephus and Philo claim that Jews in the first century AD were very interested in astrology. Josephus actually calls it a Jewish invention. However, according to him, the planets are only agents of the one true god.[55]

Even today, astrology has an odd place in Judaism. According to the Orthodox Union:

> In Judaism, Astrology is not regarded as "idol worship," even though the generic name for "idol worship" is "Avodat Kochavim U'Mazalot," Worship of the Stars and the Signs of the Zodiac."
>
> From the Jewish perspective, the stars are not unrelated to events on earth. It is not irrelevant whether one was born on Pesach, or Yom Kippur, or Lag Ba'Omer or on any particular day. Each day is special and has a unique imprint.
>
> On the other hand, if an individual was born under the "sign" of Mars, the Talmud says that he will have a tendency to spill blood. This tendency can be realized in a number of very different ways, however, which are subject to an individual's choice. In this case, options might be a soldier, a surgeon, a murderer, a "shochet," a ritual slaughterer of animals, or a "mohel," one who

---

[54] Campion (2008), p. 124.
[55] Campion (2008), pp. 121–122.

performs ritual circumcisions. These options correspond to a potential hero, a healer, one who violates the "image of G-d," to those who do "holy work" of different types.

There is a principle, "Ayn Mazal L'Yisrael," "Israel's fate is not determined by the stars." The Jew, raised in his People's traditions and Torah values, feels the reality of "freedom of choice" in his bones. So deeply ingrained is this knowledge and feeling, that the Jew rarely has cause to think about astrological factors.[56]

Figure 8. Floor of the Hamat Tiberias Synagogue [57]

The reasoning above is probably a logical consequence of the fact that the influence of the stars is mentioned in the Talmud. Instead

---

[56] See https://www.ou.org/judaism-101/resources/significance-astrology-judaism./ (read 2016-11-27)
[57] © Bukvoed on Wikipedia.com; see https://en.wikipedia.org/wiki/Hamat_Tiberias#/media/File:Hamat-Tiberias-

of trying to reconcile the Talmud with the prohibition against divination, we could say that some of the rabbis really thought it was worthwhile to consider astrological factors. That the Jews were influenced by astrology is further proved by the fact that the Sanhedrin, the Jewish Great Council, met in the third century AD at the Hamat Tiberias Synagogue, where they had an image of the zodiac on the floor (see Figure 8). The same image has been found in other synagogues, so we know that it was seen as a legitimate way of decorating a synagogue. We also know from other pictures that the centre of the zodiac had the image of a sun god in his chariot. The Jewish community was obviously not immune to astrology, and it found its way into the Talmud and the synagogues.

2.10 Astrology and the Bible

When discussing astrology and the Bible, it is important to separate three things: (1) what is a disciple of God expected to do? (2) To what extent does the Bible say that truth is revealed through the stars? (3) How do people interested in astrology perceive the Bible and what it says about the heavens?

The Bible is completely against astrology, as we saw in Chapter 2.9. That is also the view held by the early Christians, as we will see in Chapter 3.2.2. All righteous Jews as well as all righteous Christians will not exchange the word of God for interpretations of the skies or dreams. Astrology is not the way in which God talks to His people. These are the basic views in the Bible.

The Bible is aware of the use of divination in Babylon, but condemns it as useless:

> Come down, and sit in the dust, O virgin daughter of Babylon; sit on the ground; there is no throne, O daughter of the Chaldeans. For you shall no more be

---

119.jpg photo by user. Used under licence CC BY 3.0; see https://creativecommons.org/licenses/by/3.0.

> called tender and delicate. ... 13 You are wearied in the multitude of your counsels; let now the astrologers, the stargazers, the monthly prognosticators stand up and save you from these things that shall come upon you. 14 Surely they shall be as stubble, the fire shall burn them; they shall not deliver themselves from the power of the flame; it shall not be coal to be warmed by nor a fire to sit before. 15 Thus those shall be to you with whom you have labored, even your merchants, from your youth; they shall wander, everyone to his quarter. No one shall save you.[58]

However, conversely, the Bible in no way suggests that the skies absolutely cannot bring a message from God. In a psalm, the Bible says:

> 1 The heavens declare the glory of God, and the firmament shows His handiwork. 2 Day unto day utters speech, and night unto night declares knowledge. 3 There is no speech and there are no words; their voice is not heard. 4 Their line has gone out through all the earth, and their words to the end of the world. In them has He set a tent for the sun, 5 which is like a bridegroom coming out of his chamber; it rejoices as a strong man to run a race. 6 Its going forth is from one end of the heavens, and its circuit extends to the other end, and there is nothing hidden from its heat.[59]

Verse 3 here needs some clarification. The point is that there is no tongue or language where the voice of the stars cannot be heard, since the stars are seen everywhere.

In this psalm, the Bible describes how the firmament, the vault of the sky, talks to earth. The text in no way supports astrology, and

---

[58] The Bible (MEV), Isaiah 47:1,13–15.
[59] The Bible (MEV), Psalm 19:1–6.

there are many priests and pastors who have discussed the universe and heavens witnessing God, without ever thinking about or attempting to support astrology. When the Bible says that the skies talk about God, this is not the same as showing support of astrology.

A disciple of God is not supposed to use astrology, but at the same time, the disciple admits that the creation is a witness of God. The disciple should not seek God's message in astrology, but in the Holy Scriptures.

God, on the other hand, is free to use the sky as His blackboard, and to give signals to individuals as well as the people of the whole earth. According to Paul, God lets Himself be known through the skies:

> 18 The wrath of God is revealed from heaven against all ungodliness and unrighteousness of men, who suppress the truth through unrighteousness. 19 For what may be known about God is clear to them since God has shown it to them. 20 The invisible things about Him—His eternal power and deity—have been clearly seen since the creation of the world and are understood by the things that are made, so that they are without excuse. 21 Because, although they knew God, they did not glorify Him or give thanks to Him as God, but became futile in their imaginations, and their foolish hearts were darkened. 22 Claiming to be wise, they became fools. 23 They changed the glory of the incorruptible God into an image made like corruptible man, birds, four-footed beasts, and creeping things.[60]

God lets Himself be known in creation, but He should be sought in scriptures and prayers, and in churches true to His word.

---

[60] The Bible (MEV), Romans 1:18–23.

Finally, it must be acknowledged that God does let His will and intentions be known through the skies. The Star of Bethlehem is one such example. Another example is all the signs in the sky, of which Revelation is full. God forbids His disciples to use astrology, but if He chooses to use the stars to let Himself be known, that is something completely different.

The Star of Bethlehem was a sign to the heathens. The heathens are free to interpret the sign as they want, and their interpretation does not have to be the correct one.

2.11 Stars and angels in *The Book of Enoch* and in Qumran

Qumran is an archaeological site in Israel. In the second century BC and up to AD 68, it was thought to be home to a Jewish group called the Essenes, even though some scholars suggest other Jewish groups were based there, or even that it was a non-sectarian settlement.

In Qumran, some books and texts have been found showing that its inhabitants were very interested in angels. *The Book of Enoch* discusses how some of the watchers (angels) fell from God, and how they taught different skills to people, and let them know some of the secrets of heaven.

The Book of Enoch is also very interested in the stars and planets and the construction of heaven. It discusses the movements of the sun and the moon.

Somehow, there is a connection between stars and angels, even if this connection is never made clear. God is the Lord of the Hosts, which is generally taken as meaning the Lord of the Angels – but it might also refer to a host of stars:

> And beware, lest you lift up your eyes to heaven, and when you see the sun, and the moon, and the stars, even all the host of heaven, you are led astray and worship

them, and serve them, that which the Lord your God has allotted to all nations under the whole heaven.[61]

In the neighbouring cultures, the stars and planets were gods, and there was always a risk that the people would turn to them. According to the Bible, the people did so, and used the temple to worship the host of heaven:

> 4 The king [Josiah] commanded Hilkiah the high priest, the priests of the second order, and the keepers of the threshold to bring out of the temple of the Lord all the implements that were made for Baal, for Asherah, and for all the host of heaven. Then he burned them outside Jerusalem in the fields of Kidron and carried their ashes to Bethel. 5 Then he removed the idolatrous priests whom the kings of Judah had ordained to burn incense on the high places at the cities of Judah and around Jerusalem; those also who burned incense to Baal, to the sun, to the moon, to the constellations, and to all the host of heaven.[62]

Thus, the stars and planets could be seen as gods or angels. In Greco-Roman times, the Jews lived mixed in with other religions, and there was always the risk of them borrowing concepts from heathen cultures. In Judaism, the angels are supporters of God, and they occupy the same relation to God Almighty as lesser Greek gods have to Jupiter, for instance. Since the stars, to a righteous Jew, could be seen as being part of God's host, it would probably have been tempting to connect angels to the stars, especially since the word for angels means "messenger", both in Hebrew: מַלְאָךְ (malak) and Greek: ἄγγελος (angelos).

---

[61] The Bible (MEV), Deuteronomy 4:19.
[62] The Bible (MEV), 2 Kings 23:4–5.

The New Testament also relates stars to angels. In Revelation 1:19–20, stars are used as a sign for angels:

> 19 Write the things which you have seen, and the things which are, and the things which will take place after this. 20 The mystery of the seven stars which you saw in My right hand, and the seven golden candlesticks: The seven stars are the angels of the seven churches, and the seven candlesticks which you saw are the seven churches.[63]

In later Jewish texts, the planets are equated with archangels. For instance, the archangel Michael is connected to Mercury.[64] Such connections occur in the Middle Ages, but the connections resemble the ancient connections between gods and planets in the Greco-Roman world.

It is thus an open question whether such connections between individual angels in the host of the Lord were already being made in Greco-Roman times. It is plausible, but evidence is lacking. However, one connection between angels on the one hand, and planets and constellations on the other, is quite clear. It concerns the well-known images for the gospels: the angel/man, the lion, the ox and the eagle. This will be discussed further in Chapter 6.

In this book, the theory is that the fight between Archangel Michael and the seven-headed dragon/serpent in Revelation 12 can be connected to the position of the planet Mercury in June in 2 BC, which was above the constellation Hydra, a multi-headed serpent (see Chapter 7.6.5).

---

[63] The Bible (MEV), Revelation 1:19–20.
[64] See http://www.jewishencyclopedia.com/articles/10779-michael. (read 2016-11-28)

3 What was a magus to Matthew and his readers?

In the Preface, we saw that magi did exist in Babylonia and Persia. However, magi also existed in the Roman Empire. The word "magus" was a noun used in Greek, but what did it mean and how was the word used? What did Matthew intend by it and how did readers interpret his text?

3.1 Magi as officials in the Parthian Empire

The word *magus* (pl. *magi*) is the root for the current word *magician*. The Greek word goes back to an Old Persian word, *magush*, which is thought to mean "to have power" and is possibly related to the word *machine*.

3.1.1 The origin of the magi

In Chapter 4.7, we will see that the Parthian Empire was an important enemy for the Roman Empire, and that this empire lay in present-day Iran and Iraq. In this empire, the magi held an important position as diviners. They also exercised a political position when the empire needed to choose a new king.

We do not know the origin of the magi, but they seem to have originally held positions as priests in the Persian Empire. Unfortunately, Alexander the Great set fire to the capital, Persepolis, and due to this, we probably lost many documents that would have helped us understand the history and culture of Persia.

The best source for the history of the magi is thus the Greek historian Herodotus. He mentions magi in Persia, and he uses the word "magi" in two different ways: firstly to refer to an ethnic group belonging to the Medes, a geographical area in Persia; and secondly, to refer to a cast of priests. In theory, the cast of priests could be an ethnic group, but Herodotus does not say anything about the priests' ethnicity.[65]

From other sources, we know that some cultures in the ancient Near East consisted of a mixture of people with different positions in society, similar to the caste system in India. It is thus possible that the magi were once an ethnic group, having the same position in society as the Brahmin priestly cast in India.

Perhaps magi are already mentioned in the Bible where Jeremiah describes the Babylonian conquest of Jerusalem:

> All the officials of the king of Babylon entered and sat in the Middle Gate: Nergal-Sharezer, Samgar-Nebo, Sarsekim the Rabsaris Nergal-Sharezer the Rabmag, and all the rest of the officials of the king of Babylon …[66]

In this text, Nergal-Sharezer is described as "Rabmag", which could mean *Head of the magi*. However, this cannot be taken as proof that the Babylonians had magi at this time, as "Rabmag" could be interpreted differently.

The word "magi" was probably not used in Babylonia or Assyria for diviners prior to the Persian conquest. The conclusion here is that the magi originally held positions as priests and diviners in the Parthian Empire, and that they held considerable political power in the last century BC and first century AD. When Persia conquered Babylonia, the word "magi" came to be used for diviners in Babylonia.

3.1.2 The role of the magi in divination

The Persian and Parthian magi are known to have practised divination – but not divination of the stars. This might seem surprising, but we have no evidence to support the claim that they

---

[65] Zaehner (1961), p. 163.
[66] The Bible (MEV), Jeremiah 39:3.

interpreted the skies. They are known instead to have interpreted skin marks, plants and dreams.[67] This is such a well-established fact that van Kooten, in his theory about the Star of Bethlehem, actually has to suggest that the Parthian magi were influenced by Greek astrology, and that this happened because "they clearly rubbed shoulders with the Chaldean astronomers".[68]

Of course, it is possible that the Parthian magi could have become influenced by the Chaldean astronomers – that is, the Babylonian astronomers (see Chapter 3.2) – and applied Greek astronomy to events in the sky. It is up to the reader to decide how plausible this theory is.

Since the Babylonian magi obviously transferred Enuma Anu Enlil to the Mandaeans, we have reason to believe that traditional divination was practised and held in high esteem in Babylonia. Western astrology was certainly practised too, but we know very little about it. To assume that the magi of Babylon influenced their Persian colleagues also contradicts the fact that the Persian magi had a completely different view of the stars. Babylonian divination and Greek astrology contradict the Parthian magi's view of the planets according to their Zoroastrian religion (see Chapter 8.3). The planets are considered to be evil, so it is very difficult to believe that traditional divination in Babylonia was used by the Parthian magi.

Van Kooten's line of reasoning is quite strange. We have to first assume that the Chaldeans in Babylon practised Greek astrology, and then assume that the magi of Parthia borrowed astrology from the Chaldeans. These assumptions are completely without support from any written source from the time; neither is there any support for assuming that Persian/Parthian magi practised divination of the stars. But there is evidence suggesting the opposite, that they were against any form of divination of the stars.

---

[67] Ossendrijver (2015), pp. 225–226.
[68] van Kooten (2015), pp. 499, 594.

3.2 Chaldeans and the magi

When Alexander the Great conquered Mesopotamia and entered the city of Babylon, he was greeted by the people. In AD 50, the Roman historian Quintus Curtius Rufus described how Alexander was greeted in his book, *History of Alexander*:

> Next came the magi chanting a song in their native fashion, and behind them were the Chaldeans (Chaldei), who were not only the diviners (vates) of the Babylonians but also musicians equipped with their typical instruments. The role of the latter was to sing the praises of the kings, that of the Chaldeans to reveal the motions of the stars and the regular change of the seasons.[69]

Rufus here makes a distinction between the magi and the Chaldeans, who are seen as diviners. In other texts, the Chaldeans are seen as the native inhabitants of southern Babylonia,[70] and in other texts, the word "magi" is used in a more general sense denoting foreign scholars from Mesopotamia and Persia/Parthia.[71]

The Chaldeans had a great reputation in the Greek and Roman era as diviners. This was because they predicted the death of Alexander the Great:

> While he was still three hundred furlongs from the city, the scholars called Chaldeans, who have gained a great reputation in astrology and are accustomed to predict future events by a method based on old-aged observations, chose from their number the eldest and most experienced. By the prophetic power of the stars (ton asteron manteias), they had learned of the coming death of the king of Babylon, and they instructed their

---

[69] Ossendrijver (2015), p. 217.
[70] van Kooten (2015), p. 619.
[71] Ossendrijver (2015), pp. 225–226.

representatives to report to the king the danger which threatened.[72]

Due to this, many magi in the Roman Empire claimed to be Chaldeans and offered their services to customers. In other words, magi were known to travel around in the Roman Empire, and magi were often seen as Chaldeans, though not always. As a result of this, we cannot tell by the word alone if Matthew intended "magi" to mean Chaldean astrologers, diviners in general, or Parthian priests and court officials.

However, it is quite clear that Matthew intended them to be "diviners coming from the east." To press this further and decide that he "must have meant magi from Parthia" or any other more specific conclusion, is nonsensical.

Perhaps Matthew used an imprecise word because he did not know the exact origin of the magi. Researchers who claim to know exactly what Matthew meant are merely deceiving themselves.

3.2.1 Magi as diviners, magicians and sorcerers

People who engage in divination – be it by the stars, dreams, plants, or skin marks – are often seen with scepticism by others. The word "magi" was thus often used in a negative sense in the Greek and Roman world.

Van Kooten discusses how the word was used, arguing that the magi were seen as a positive force up to the time of Emperor Nero (AD 54–68). During Nero's time as emperor, an Armenian king called Tiridates, of Parthian descent, travelled to Rome. Tiridates was also a magus and went to Rome to get Nero's blessing for his kingship. It is said that he travelled by land on horseback with three thousand equestrians through Syria and Greece and all the way to Rome.[73] According to van Kooten, many people witnessed this trip.

---

[72] Ossendrijver (2015), p. 221.
[73] van Kooten (2015), p. 571.

He suggests that this trip might have given the early Christians the idea that Christ too was visited by magi.

After Nero, however, van Kooten believes that the attitude to magi turned from positive to negative, and continued to worsen thereafter. Van Kooten cites Acts 13:6–8:

> 6 When they had gone through the whole island to Paphos, they found a certain sorcerer, a Jewish false prophet, whose name was Bar-Jesus, 7 who was with the proconsul, Sergius Paulus, an intelligent man. This man called for Barnabas and Saul and sought to hear the word of God. 8 But Elymas the sorcerer (which is his name by interpretation) opposed them, trying to divert the proconsul from the faith. 9 Then Saul, who also is called Paul, filled with the Holy Spirit, stared at him and said, 10 "You son of the devil, enemy of all righteousness, full of deceit and of all fraud, will you not cease perverting the right ways of the Lord? 11 Now, look! The hand of the Lord is against you, and you shall be blind, not seeing the sun for a time."[74]

In the text above, the word "magus" is translated as *sorcerer*. Van Kooten sees this as proof that the use of the word had changed. In short, van Kooten believes that during the time of Augustus and up to the time of Nero, magi were seen in a positive sense and in connection with Parthian court officials, and thus, this is what Matthew meant when he used the word. After Nero, its meaning changed, and became something negative: a despised sorcerer.[75]

This book strongly disagrees with van Kooten's views. Rome had a population of 50–60 million people, and many of them spoke Greek as their native language or to communicate with strangers. There was no Internet, no books, no newspapers and no television, so the

---

[74] The Bible (MEV), Acts 13:6–8.
[75] van Kooten (2015), p. 585.

Greek language was learnt by word of mouth, and the meaning and usage of words was very stable. The word "magi" was not used very much, as magi were not a common topic of discussion among people. Under such circumstances, the meaning of a word will be stable. "Magi" was used interchangeably with "Chaldeans" and they were thought of as diviners of some sort, or foreign scholars. People could use the word positively, negatively or neutrally depending on their attitude to divination or foreign scholars.

Further, van Kooten does not take into account that the main sources available to us from Roman times are historical and political sources. Since Rome and Parthia were in ongoing conflicts and alliances with each other, and since the magi were court officials in Parthia, it is natural that our Greek and Roman sources would mention the magi as Parthian court officials and in a neutral, positive or negative sense depending on the current political relations between the two parties. It would not mean that everyone in the Roman world would have used the word "magi" in that sense; it is just how our sources use the word.

Ordinary people are very likely to have used the word in different ways depending on how they personally viewed the magi. Matthew used it in a positive sense, because his magi play a positive role. This does not prove that Matthew saw the magi as Parthian court officials. In fact, we must ask ourselves how likely it is that Matthew was aware of Roman foreign relations and the titles of visiting foreign representatives.

In Europe, we often know the title of the highest politician in a neighbouring country. We seldom know other titles high up in the hierarchy, and this is despite being able to see foreign politicians occasionally in the media. In the Greco-Roman world there was no form of media that could be used as a source of information. To assume that Matthew had knowledge about court officials in a foreign country is thus a bold assumption.

It would be very strange if he were unaware that the word "magi" was connected to sorcerers and magicians. He probably knew that the word could be used in such a way, but also that it could be used for diviners. In the context, he probably means diviners of the Chaldean sort. Matthew does not criticise divination as such; he simply wants to tell us that magi arrived in Bethlehem when Christ was an infant. He could have thought that the magi were from Babylon, since Babylonia and Chaldea were synonyms, but he does not mention this. The logical conclusion is, therefore, that we cannot say where the magi came from according to Matthew, apart from his statement that they came from the east; and perhaps Matthew wrote that they came from the east because that was the only thing he knew about their origins. However, it is also possible that he mentioned the east because he wanted to be clear that the magi were not from the Greco-Roman area.

3.2.2 Magi in the early Church

The early Church connected the magi with Balaam in Numbers 24:17. As we saw above, some late Jewish kings and military leaders from the second century BC to the second century AD used Balaam's prophecy about "a star coming out of Jacob" to refer to themselves (see Chapter 2.9).

Van Kooten rightly argues that Matthew is careful to point out when a prophecy in the Old Testament has been fulfilled through Christ. Matthew does not do this at all concerning the story about the magi.[76] If Matthew had meant the story about the magi to be a fulfilment of Balaam's prophecy, he would almost certainly have written this. The connection with Balaam, however, seems to be a later interpretation, and the first attempt to connect the visit of the magi to a prophecy in the Old Testament. Justin Martyr and Irenaeus of Lyon were among those advocating this explanation. Irenaeus writes:

---

[76] van Kooten (2015), pp. 605, 617.

And again, as Moses says, "A star will rise out of Jacob, and a leader shall spring up from Israel" (Num. 24:17), clearly announcing that the dispensation of His coming into being according to the flesh would be among the Jews; and from Jacob and of the Jewish race He who was born, coming down from heaven, took up the dispensation so laid down. For the star appears in heaven; and "leader" means king, for he is King of all the saved. But the star appeared at His birth to those men, the magi, who dwelt in the East, and through it they learned that Christ was born; and led by the same star they came to Judea, till the star reached Bethlehem.[77]

In the third century, Origin continued to discuss the connection between Balaam and the magi, who he saw had contact with daemons, but the daemons did not lead them to Christ:

> For if Balaam's prophecies were introduced by Moses into the sacred books, how much more were they copied by those who were living at that time in Mesopotamia, among which Balaam had a great reputation and who are known to have been disciples of his art? After all, it is reported that from him a race and institution of magicians flourished in parts of the East, which possessed copies among themselves of everything that Balaam had prophesised. They even possessed the following writing: "A star will rise out of Jacob, and a man will spring from Israel" (Numbers 24:7 LXX) (*sic*) [should be 24:17]. The magi had these writings among themselves, and that is why, when Jesus was born, they recognized the star and they understood, more than the people of Israel, who

---

[77] Hannah (2015), p. 436.

despised hearing the words of the holy prophets, that the prophecy was being fulfilled. Therefore, based only on the writings that Balaam had left behind, when they knew that the time was near, they came looking for him, and immediately worshiped him. And to declare the greatness of their faith, they venerated the small child as a king.[78]

In the fifth or sixth century, a text called *Arabic Infancy Gospel* was written, probably in Syria. In this text, Balaam is exchanged with Zoroaster, the founder of Zoroastrianism. The text says that it was Zoroaster who "predicted the advent of Christ: his birth from a virgin, his career, death, resurrection, and ascension".[79]

3.3 Conclusion

In short, the early Christians did not know why the magi came, nor did they know what star or what kind of star the magi had seen. Matthew's text could not give them any direction, and the early tradition focused on Balaam.

When the New Testament was translated into Latin, the problematic word *magi* was translated as *wise men*, which was probably the best translation, since it reflects the positive attitude Matthew had towards them. Also, the term "wise men" still suggests they have special knowledge, but not in connection with sorcery.

---

[78] Hannah (2015), pp. 438–439, 441.
[79] Hannah (2015), pp. 450–451.

4 Political history in the Middle East

In order to perform a critical analysis of the story of the Star of Bethlehem, we need to understand the general political history of the surrounding area, as well as its cultural and religious development. In fact, we need to go back to the third millennium BC. The reason that such a large focus is needed is that Mesopotamian culture was rather stable for more than two millennia, and to some extent it survived a couple of hundred years into the first millennium AD. Babylonian scribes preserved texts, historical details and religious beliefs going back to the third millennium BC, and in order to understand how the magi interpreted the signs, we need to take into consideration how they dealt with the different traditions they had preserved from the different phases of Mesopotamia.

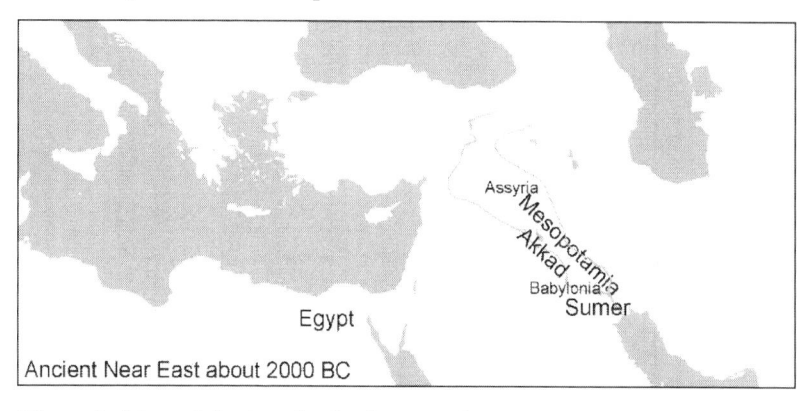

Figure 9. Map of the first flood cultures and subsequent countries

We shall therefore now look at the political history of the Middle East in order to be acquainted with the general devolvement of states and empires in the area (see Figure 9). This will serve as a background for examining its cultural and religious history in the next chapter.

4.1 The rise of the Egyptian and Mesopotamian flood cultures

The oldest civilisations in this part of the world emerged in Egypt and Mesopotamia. Both names are of Greek origin, although the Greek word for Egypt can be traced back to the Egyptian name of a temple in Memphis. Mesopotamia means *between the rivers*.

Both of these countries emerged on the fertile soil created by the yearly flooding of the rivers: the Nile in Egypt and the Euphrates and the Tigris in Mesopotamia. In both countries, a centralised government arose in the third millennium BC. Egypt had a good strategic position, since it was protected by deserts to the east and west. A central government could emerge without serious threats from the surrounding areas, and soon one dynasty controlled the whole area.

In Mesopotamia, the situation was completely different. The original inhabitants in southern Mesopotamia seem to have been the Sumerians, a people who called themselves *Black heads*. We do not know if this had anything to do with hair or skin colour. The Sumerians dominated the third millennium BC, and developed the cuneiform script. However, due to decreasing rainfall, people from the surrounding areas immigrated to Sumer over the centuries. The new arrivals generally spoke Semitic languages, and after some time, the Sumerians became a minority in their own country.

Due to pressure from abroad, it was difficult for any Sumerian city state to dominate the others. The King of Kish was the formal title for the overlord of the entire Sumerian area, and the local dynasties seem to have competed to secure this title for themselves. The history of the area in the third millennium BC is not very well known, which is a great shame, since so much of our own culture is indebted to this early civilisation.

4.2 The Akkadian Empire and the first Assyrian and Babylonian kingdoms

In around 2300 BC, the whole of Mesopotamia was united for the first time under Sargon of Akkad, a Semitic-speaking ruler. From this time, the area became known as Akkad, which included the northern as well as the southern part of Mesopotamia (see Figure 9 on page 63). Over the course of the following millennia, the area developed into several different states with different names, but the name Akkad continued to be an archaic term for the whole area, even if from time to time it was divided into different competing states. The language of the area is known as Akkadian, and since the society was a literate, continuous society with written religious texts and other documents, the language continued to be used up to the first millennium AD.

The Akkadian Empire only lasted a couple of centuries before it fell apart. In northern Mesopotamia, an Assyrian kingdom rose in the early second millennium BC. This was soon followed by the Old Babylonian kingdom in the south. Semitic-speaking people dominated both countries, and the Sumerian population was absorbed. Hammurabi the Great seized power in Babylon in the early eighteenth century BC. Hammurabi failed to conquer Assyria completely, but Assyria became a vassal state. Then, in the sixteenth century BC, an invading army of unknown origin sacked Babylon, and the Babylonian Empire fell apart.

The fall of Babylon made it possible for the Kassites to conquer the area. The original homeland of the Kassites is not known, but northern Iran has been suggested. The Kassites brought horses with them to the area, which changed warfare and resulted in an unstable political situation in the Middle East.

The climate also seems to have changed at around this time, and in the eleventh and twelfth centuries BC the Middle East saw large migrations of people. As a result, Babylonia was again invaded by people of unknown origin, and the Kassite dynasty fell.

4.3 The Neo-Assyrian and Neo-Babylonian Empires

In the early tenth century BC, the Neo-Assyrian Empire emerged and conquered Mesopotamia, and in the following centuries large parts of present-day Syria and the northern part of present-day Israel, while Judah was not conquered. In its backyard, the Neo-Babylonian kingdom arose in the late seventh century under Nabopolassar, who conquered Assyria. His son, Nebuchadnezzar II, conquered Judah and Egypt, and deported many Jews to Babylonian captivity in the summer of 587 or 586 BC.

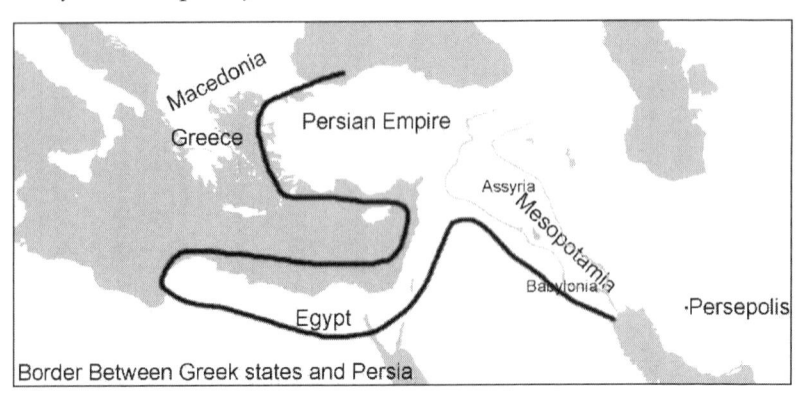

Figure 10. The Persian border at the beginning of Alexander the Great's reign in the fourth century BC.

4.4 The Persian Empire

The Babylonian Empire eventually collapsed internally, and in the middle of the sixth century BC it was conquered by Cyrus II of Persia, also called Cyrus the Great. He was a wise ruler who let several different peoples, including the Jews, return to their home countries after they had been relocated by the Babylonians.

The Persian Empire then expanded rapidly and conquered Egypt in the late sixth century BC. In the early fifth century, Persia began to threaten Greek city states in present-day Turkey (see Figure 10).

4.5 The rise of the Greeks and Alexander the Great

In the fourth century BC, the Macedonian king Philip II formed a league between most Greek city states to fight against Persia, but he was killed in 336 BC. As a result, Persia then controlled present-day Iran and Iraq, large parts of present-day Turkey, Syria, Lebanon, Israel and Egypt, and the south Mediterranean coastal area. The Greeks thus now faced a mighty foe with much greater military strength.

After Philip II died, the Persian king Darius III attacked Philip's son, Alexander (later to be known as Alexander the Great). Alexander fought back, and in a few years he defeated the Persians in present-day Turkey, Syria, Israel and Egypt. On 1st October 331 BC the Persians also suffered a major defeat at Gaugamela, close to what is now Mosul in northern Iraq. Soon afterwards, the Babylonians travelled to the victorious Alexander the Great and offered him the city of Babylon.

Darius III was killed by one of his own satraps (governors), who took Darius' throne. The usurper was in turn defeated and executed by Alexander the following year. Alexander burnt the Persian capital Persepolis in 330 BC. Alexander had defeated his enemy totally, and Greeks settled in cities all over the conquered area.

In 323 BC Alexander died in Babylon at the age of 33. Ten years of internal struggles for power among Alexander's generals followed. The outcome was that the generals managed to secure different parts of Alexander's empire for themselves. Seleucus gained Mesopotamia and Persia for himself, while Ptolemy secured Egypt.

The death of Alexander the Great was also in fact the deathblow for the old city of Babylon, which it seems had been intended to be the capital of his empire. However, in 305 BC Seleucus founded Seleucia, a new capital situated about sixty kilometres to the north of Babylon, on the west bank of the Tigris. Eventually this new city would depopulate Babylon, and would be filled with Greek-speaking people who did not maintain the old Mesopotamian traditions.

Alexander the Great and the magi in Babylon had had a good relationship; he had planned to rebuild the temples and restore Babylon to its former glory. However, in just twenty years or so, the magi found that the death of Alexander meant that they were going to be cast aside.

The state of affairs at the end of the first millennium BC was that Babylon was in decay, and the power and influence of the original inhabitants of Mesopotamia, as well as their religion, were on the wane. Babylon was falling into ruin.

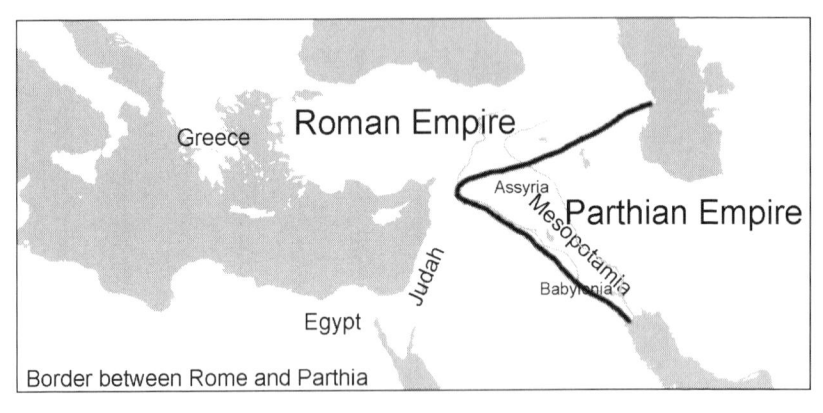

Figure 11. The eastern part of the Roman Empire in the first century BC

4.6 The Roman Empire

While the Greeks were busy defeating Persia and dividing the spoils of Alexander the Great's victories, Italy saw the rise of the Roman Empire. In the second and first centuries BC, the Romans conquered Greece and large parts of present-day Syria and Israel. In Egypt, the Ptolemaic dynasty fell with Queen Cleopatra (see Figure 11).

4.7 The Parthian Empire

In Persia, the Parthian Empire was established in the second century BC. It took advantage of Roman expansion and wars against the Greeks. The Parthians soon conquered Mesopotamia, and in the first century BC, they even successfully fought against the Romans. At the turn of the millennium, Mesopotamia was dominated by Parthians.

Parthia was an unstable empire, and princes fought each other to gain the crown. But when the Romans tried to take advantage of such internal struggles by attacking Parthia, the Parthians united and fought back against the Romans. In response, the Romans then chose to expand their influence in Parthia by supporting different princes in the struggle for power, but they failed to defeat the Parthian Empire as such.

Mesopotamia remained outside the Roman Empire, even though the Romans occasionally conquered parts of it. When Christ was born, Rome and Parthia were at peace with one another, and we know that scientists from Rome were able to travel around in the Parthian Empire. Presumably, Parthians could travel around the Roman Empire in the same way. Thus, there is no historical reason to question the conclusion that the magi could have travelled from the Parthian Empire into the Roman Empire.

4.8 Judah (Judea)

Judah (or 'Judea' in Latin) lay between the Seleucid and Ptolemaic kingdoms, and wars continued to rage in the area. Occasionally, local Jewish princes succeeded in establishing a pact with one of the competing Greek kingdoms, at which point another Greek kingdom would soon support that prince's rival. Independence and safety could not be secured.

When the Romans turned their interest to the eastern shores of the Mediterranean, they supported Herod the Great in his struggle to become king of Judah. The Parthians supported another candidate, however, and they were initially successful in installing this new king in power in Judah. Meanwhile, Herod formed an alliance with the Roman general Mark Antony (see Chapter 9.5) and together they forced out the new Parthian king and secured Judah for Herod.

Herod the Great was a friend of Emperor Augustus, but in the last years of Herod's reign, he lost this status. The reason seems to have been that Herod started a minor war against a minor king in Arabia, a king who had the support of Parthia. Such a war threatened the peace that Augustus had been striving to uphold with Parthia, and the friendship was lost.[80]

When Herod died, his kingdom was split between three of his sons, who were not called kings but ethnarchs. The son named Archelaus, mentioned in Matthew 2:22, became ethnarch of Judah, Samaria and Idumea, while his brother, Herod Antipas, ruled Galilee and Perea, a third son, Philip got Iturea and Trachonitis in the northeast. By the year AD 6, Archelaus had become so unpopular that he was deposed by Emperor Augustus and banished to southern France. As a result, Judah came under the direct control of the Roman Empire and officially lost its independence, although it had already effectively lost its independence during King Herod's time. King Herod and his sons as well as Quirinius will be discussed in more detail later (see Chapter 9).

Herod Antipas continued to reign in Galilee until AD 39. During Passover, Christ was sent to Herod Antipas by Pontius Pilate for

---

[80] van Kooten (2015), p. 550.

trial, since Christ came from Galilee, but Antipas sent him back to Pontius Pilate.

The first half of the first century AD was relatively peaceful, since Rome in practice dominated the area. However, in the second half of the first century AD there was a turn for the worse, and a Jewish revolt against the Romans began. In AD 70, the revolt ended with the second destruction of the temple of Jerusalem. During this revolt, approximately one million Jews were killed and two hundred thousand were enslaved. Finally, in the year AD 135, the Jews lost yet another revolt, and were consequently evicted from Jerusalem and banned from entering it again.

There is no proof of Christian involvement in the defence of Jerusalem in the year AD 70. According to tradition, the Christians had left the city in advance due to a prophecy about the fall of the city.

5 The cultural and religious development of Mesopotamia

If the magi came from Babylonia, it is important to take a deeper look at the cultural and religious development of Mesopotamia. This chapter builds on the general and political developments of Mesopotamia and neighbouring areas examined in Chapters 2–4.

5.1 The status of Sumerian culture

The Sumerians invented the cuneiform script, which was written on clay tablets. Large libraries have been found in Mesopotamia, making it possible for us to follow the political and religious developments of the time. The ancient inhabitants of Mesopotamia were aware that these libraries existed, and ancient kings conducted excavations in order to recover old texts. The Semitic intellectuals of Babylonia and Assyria valued old texts highly, and age was considered a sign of quality.

In the third century BC, Berossos, a priest and magus belonging to the god Marduk's temple in Babylon, either emigrated or was brought as a prisoner to the Greek Island of Kos[81] (see Chapter 2.7). He brought Babylonian culture to the Greeks, such as showing them a translation of the Sumerian myth about the Great Flood. The Babylonians had their own versions of the Flood story, but Berossos favoured the older, Sumerian version, and chose not to use the later, Babylonian Gilgamesh epic.

In Mesopotamia, Sumerian culture held the same elevated status that Roman/Latin culture held in Western cultures in more modern times, and a Babylonian intellectual was expected to learn Sumerian.

---

[81] von Stuckrad (2015), p. 390.

5.2 The Sumerian gods

The Sumerians had many different gods, but the main gods were Anu, Enki, Enlil and Ninhursag. The word An means *heaven* or *sky*, and An was the king of heaven. Enlil means *Lord of the sky*, and he was the god of the atmosphere. Enki possibly means *Lord of the earth*, and he was later known as Ea, which is thought to have originally have been the name of his temple in the Sumerian city Eridu. Ninhursag was the fertility goddess. In the first millennium BC, she was connected with the Virgin constellation.

Another important god was Ninurta, the god of hunting. He was particularly popular in the late Assyrian kingdom, and he was associated with the planet Saturn. His father was Enlil, and his mother was sometimes thought to be Ninhursag.

Ninurta was the hero of Sumerian literature, and many of the stories connected to him are later attributed to the Greek hero Hercules. One of the myths describes how he killed the seven-headed dragon/serpent, which corresponds to Hercules slaying the Hydra. This fight against the dragon was later attributed to the Babylonian god Marduk, and later to Marduk's son, Nabu, then also to the archangel Michael and St George (see Chapter 7.6.5).

When Ninurta killed the dragon, he wound the serpent around a beam of his chariot. A snake around a pole is thus, originally, a sign of Ninurta. This sign is today the rod of Asclepius, the Greek and Roman god of medicine and healing, used as a sign for medicine and physicians. This is logical, since in Ninurta's struggle against evil, he is also the bringer of health.

Another symbol for Ninurta was the eagle, probably because in another myth, he killed an evil eagle. The eagle sometimes has two heads, and it is possible that this motif is the backdrop for the use of double-headed eagles in the coats of arms of leading families in the Holy Roman Empire and the Russian Empire. The symbol originated in Mesopotamia and was incorporated as an imperial attribute in eastern Rome, and from there it seems to have been borrowed by the imperial dynasties in Austria (the Holy Roman Empire) and the Russian Empire.

Apart from Ninhursag and Ninurta, the other Sumerian gods were not associated with planets, stars or constellations, but with the night sky more generally. This is quite natural, since divination was developed a thousand years after the height of Sumerian culture. The connection between the gods Ninhursag and Ninurta and the stars was probably not made in Sumerian times.

Contrary to what we might think about an agricultural society, the sun only played a minor role in the pantheon, and was called Utu.

5.3 The Old Babylonian gods

Hammurabi made the city of Babylon the centre of his kingdom and Marduk was the patron deity of Babylon; so with the rise of the Babylonian Empire, Marduk rose to be the highest god. His name is thought to mean *Bull calf of Utu*, and since Utu was a sun god, Marduk was the calf of the sun god. In the night sky, he was represented by the constellation Taurus and the planet Jupiter.

To match his new status as the principal god, a new creation myth called Enuma Elish was written, in which Marduk was the main creator of the world. He created the world by killing a huge dragon/serpent.

Another important god in Babylonia was Nergal, the god of the Netherworld. He was represented by the constellation Leo and the planet Mars. As the god of pestilence, disease and the threat of war, he was the opposite of Ninurta. In Greece, the situation was the other way around: Saturn stood for 'bad' wars, betrayal and death, while Mars was the 'good' god of war. Ishtar was the female goddess of fertility, and she was represented by the planet Venus.

In the second millennium BC, a minor role was played by Nabu, Marduk's son. He was the god of scribes and record-keeping. He had no symbol of his own and was simply portrayed as a winged man; he was represented by the planet Mercury.

5.4 The Assyrian Gods

In Assyria, the main gods were Ashur and Ninurta. Ashur was the equivalent of Enlil, and in the Assyrian version of the creation of the world, Ashur played the role of Marduk.

5.5 The Neo- and Late Babylonian pantheon

When Babylonia returned to power, early in the first millennium BC, the old gods of Babylonia rose to prominence again. However, some things changed. Ninurta became Marduk's son, and Nabu rose in importance. The originally rather dull Nabu became a war god and eventually the leading god, while Marduk was rather inactive, although he was still considered to be the highest in rank. Nebuchadnezzar, who conquered Jerusalem in 586 BC, was named after Nabu.

6 The Babylonian gods and the signs of the gospels

In Christian art, the gospels are represented by a man (sometimes winged), a bull, a lion and an eagle (see Figure 12). These figures are identical to the symbols used for Nabu, Marduk, Nergal and Ninurta, respectively.

Figure 12. The signs of the gospels [82]

6.1 Ezekiel and the four-faced creatures

Many readers will probably be surprised to hear that these symbols were borrowed from Babylonia. The history behind this is that the prophet Ezekiel, in his first chapter, writes about God's throne being held in the sky by four winged creatures with four faces each.

---

[82] Photograph of door portal at St Trophime in Arles, France. © Keith Hall; used with permission obtained on 25th October 2016.

These faces happen to be the same as the symbols for the four different gods.[83] Ezekiel took these symbols into the Jewish faith.

One interpretation is that Ezekiel wanted to present God as the supreme god and show that the main gods of Babylonia served him, by carrying his throne. Another interpretation is that the creatures are winds from the four corners of the world. The four faces represent their ability to turn in any direction, and thus the faces represent north, west, east and south.

> 4 As I looked, a whirlwind came out of the north, a great cloud with fire flashing forth continually, and a brightness was all around it, and in its midst something as glowing metal in the midst of the fire. 5 Also out of the midst came the likeness of four living creatures. And this was their appearance: They had the likeness of a man. 6 Every one had four faces, and everyone had four wings. 7 Their legs were straight and the soles of their feet were like the sole of a calf's hoof. And they gleamed like the color of burnished bronze. 8 They had the hands of a man under their wings on their four sides. As for the faces and wings of the four of them, 9 their wings were joined to one another. Their faces did not turn when they went. Each went straight forward. 10 As for the likeness of their faces, each had the face of a man, and all four had the face of a lion on the right side, and the face of an ox on the left side, and the face of an eagle. 11 Thus were their faces.[84]

It is beyond the scope of this book to investigate the real background to Ezekiel's creatures. It is sufficient to note that there is a link between the symbols of these four gods and the symbols for the gospels. Ezekiel's purpose was surely not to include

---

[83] Peterson (2012), p. 119.
[84] The Bible (MEV), Ezekiel 1:4–11.

Babylonian gods into the Jewish faith, and the four creatures have never been seen as such. But for some reason, these creatures were noticed by the early Christians, and they reappear in Revelation.

6.2 Revelation and the four living creatures

In Revelation 4, John the Presbyter[85] describes four living creatures around the throne of God. These creatures resemble the creatures in Ezekiel, but with one major difference: instead of each creature having four faces, they are described as having one face each. This seems more correct when they are seen in relation to the original gods represented by the creatures.

> 6 In the midst of the throne, and around the throne, were four living creatures covered with eyes in front and in back. 7 The first living creature was like a lion, the second living creature like a calf, the third living creature had a face like a man, and the fourth creature was like a flying eagle. 8 The four living creatures had six wings each, and they were covered with eyes all around.[86]

John the Presbyter's description is thus more true to the original situation in Babylonia, where each face belonged to one separate god. In the same chapter, John the Presbyter also mentions twenty-four elders around the throne and seven lamps of fire, which are the seven spirits of God. This could be compared with later cabbalistic ideas where the seven luminaries – the sun, the moon, Mercury, Venus, Mars, Jupiter and Saturn – are connected to angels; these seven luminaries in turn represent the seven days of the week. The

---

[85] In the first chapter of Revelation, the book is said to be written by "John". The early Church was not sure if John the Evangelist or John the Presbyter was intended by this. Moreover, John the Presbyter might be another name for John the Evangelist. We shall discuss this in Chapter 10, but for now, this book simply uses the name John the Presbyter for the author of Revelation.
[86] The Bible (MEV), Revelation 4:6–8.

twenty-four elders could be thought of as the twelve hours of the day and the twelve hours of the night.

The four creatures would fit into a general celestial pattern, if they were thought of as planets and constellations. In fact, Ninurta and Nabu are connected to constellations too, so perhaps the four creatures could be seen as constellations, and the eyes could be seen as stars.

It is possible to maintain that John the Presbyter was interested in astrology and that Revelation contains astrology; since some people are interested in finding evidence of ideas that run contrary to Christian belief, such thoughts will certainly arise. However, John the Presbyter probably saw how, rather than being agents of heathen gods, the heavenly objects and time as such served God. Therefore, since Revelation is a prophecy about the future, everything connected with time would be serving God in his main plan for the world.

At any rate, John the Presbyter is more true to the original four characters than Ezekiel, who disconnected the creatures from the gods by giving each creature four faces. In Chapter 10 we will discuss John more thoroughly, but for now it is sufficient to say that the four creatures he describes fit into a pattern of stars and constellations, and are probably connected to Ezekiel's original creatures.

John the Presbyter brings Ezekiel's creatures up in Revelation, but he does not connect them to the gospels. Indeed, he could not have done so, or intended them to be connected to the gospels, since not all of the four gospels were written when Revelation was completed. Thus, the four creatures must have been important to John the Presbyter for some other reason. The theory in this book is that the four creatures were important because the sign the magi saw included the Lion, the Bull, Mercury and Saturn. If this was the case, these signs would automatically bring Ezekiel and his creatures to mind, and it would explain John the Presbyter's great interest in Ezekiel.

6.3 Irenaeus of Lyon and the four creatures

The first person known to have connected the gospels to the four creatures is St Irenaeus, who was born in Smyrna in about AD 130 and died as a martyr in AD 202. He was a pupil of Polykarpus, the bishop of Smyrna, who in turn was said to have been the pupil of John.

In Irenaeus' book *Adversus Haereses*, that is, *Against Heresies*, he writes about some important matters in the early Church. One problem at that time were the Gnostics, who emphasised secret knowledge and mysterious teachings in a battle between good and evil. They exerted influence on the Church, and the Church tried to keep the Gnostic teachings out.

Among the things discussed in the Church at that time was what books should be used. Irenaeus was a strong advocate of the four gospels, and he wrote of the four-faced creatures:

> From which fact, it is evident that the Word, the Artificer of all, He that sitteth upon the cherubim, and contains all things, He who was manifested to men, has given us the Gospel under four aspects, but bound together by one Spirit. As also David says, when entreating His manifestation, "Thou that sittest between the cherubim, shine forth." (6) For the cherubim, too, were four-faced, and their faces were images of the dispensation of the Son of God. For, [as the Scripture] says, "The first living creature was like a lion," (7) symbolizing His effectual working, His leadership, and royal power; the second [living creature] was like a calf, signifying [His] sacrificial and sacerdotal order; but "the third had, as it were, the face as of a man," – an evident description of His advent as a

human being; "the fourth was like a flying eagle," pointing out the gift of the Spirit hovering with His wings over the Church. And therefore the Gospels are in accord with these things, among which Christ Jesus is seated. For that according to John relates His original, effectual, and glorious generation from the Father, thus declaring, "In the beginning was the Word, and the Word was with God, and the Word was God." (8) Also, "all things were made by Him, and without Him was nothing made." For this reason, too, is that Gospel full of all confidence, for such is His person. (9) But that according to Luke, taking up [His] priestly character, commenced with Zacharias the priest offering sacrifice to God. For now was made ready the fatted calf, about to be immolated for (10) the finding again of the younger son. Matthew, again, relates His generation as a man, saying, "The book of the generation of Jesus Christ, the son of David, the son of Abraham;" (11) and also, "The birth of Jesus Christ was on this wise." This, then, is the Gospel of His humanity; (12) for which reason it is, too, that [the character of] a humble and meek man is kept up through the whole Gospel. Mark, on the other hand, commences with [a reference to] the prophetical spirit coming down from on high to men, saying, "The beginning of the Gospel of Jesus Christ, as it is written in Esaias the prophet," – pointing to the winged aspect of the Gospel; and on this account he made a compendious and cursory narrative, for such is the prophetical character. And the Word of God Himself used to converse with the ante-Mosaic patriarchs, in accordance with His divinity and glory; but for those under the law he instituted a sacerdotal and liturgical service. Afterwards, being made man for us, He sent the gift of the celestial Spirit over all the

> earth, protecting us with His wings. Such, then, as was the course followed by the Son of God, so was also the form of the living creatures; and such as was the form of the living creatures, so was also the character of the Gospel. For the living creatures are quadriform, and the Gospel is quadriform, as is also the course followed by the Lord.[87]

Irenaeus of Lyon is here the first recorded person to connect the gospels to the creatures, and he connects them originally to Ezekiel's creatures. As we see, he differs slightly from the normal order of the creatures. He connects the Gospel of John to the lion and the Gospel of Mark to the eagle. Today, the eagle normally represents the Gospel of John, while Mark is represented by the lion.

Jerome (c. 347–420) has another explanation, probably influenced by his contemporary Epiphanius:

> The book of Ezekiel demonstrates that these four Gospels had been predicted much earlier. Its first vision has the following description: "And in the midst there was a likeness of four animals. Their countenances were the face of a man and the face of a lion and the face of a calf and the face of an eagle." The first face of a man represents Matthew, who began his narrative as though about a man: "The book of the generation of Jesus Christ the son of David, the son of Abraham." The second, Mark, in whom the voice of a lion roaring in the wilderness is heard: "A voice of one shouting in the desert: Prepare the way of the Lord; make His paths straight." The third, of the calf, which prefigures that the evangelist Luke began with Zacharias the priest. The fourth, John the evangelist, who, having taken up

---

[87] Irenaeus, Book III, Chapter 11:8.

eagle's wings and hastening toward higher matters, discusses the Word of God.[88]

This explanation was later supported by St Augustine, and is the official explanation accepted in Western churches.

A critical analysis shows that the symbols originally had nothing to do with the gospels. For some reason, Irenaeus believed that the four creatures witnessed the coming of Christ, and he somehow came up with the idea that each creature represented a gospel. Anyone who tries to find out why or how the gospels are connected to the creatures is likely to find the connection a bit strained. We really have to read the creatures into the text, and this is probably what Irenaeus did.

An alternative interpretation is that Ezekiel's book is a prophecy about Christ, and that the coming of God to Jerusalem, described by Ezekiel, symbolises Christ coming to Jerusalem, descending from Heaven and being presented to us through the four creatures. Some maintain that the Gospel of John is written in such a way that it reflects Ezekiel.[89] We shall look into this further in Chapter 10.4.

To make the connection work, Irenaeus connects the creatures to episodes in each gospel, while Jerome and Epiphanius concentrate on the beginnings of each gospel. However, it is obvious that the four creatures have been read into the text to make them fit to the "one creature each" pattern.

The theory in this book is that Irenaeus was aware that the four creatures witnessed the coming of Christ. He had learned this tradition from John, via Polykarpus, but the original connection to the stars had been lost in transition. He then later connected these signs to the gospels.

---

[88] Scheck (2008), pp. 55–56.
[89] Peterson (2015).

7 Astronomical events suggested to be the Star of Bethlehem

In this chapter, we shall examine previous attempts to identify the Star of Bethlehem. We shall also examine what critics have said about these theories.

7.1 The sceptical view

It is always a good idea to take into account what sceptics say. Many people treat the story as an invention – pure fiction. Some believe the story has a kernel of truth, and others believe every detail.

The most sceptical view is that the early Christians invented the story in the second half of the first century AD. In the year AD 66, a procession of magi travelled from Armenia to Rome to visit Emperor Nero, as discussed earlier. This procession might have been seen by several Christian communities in the northeast corner of the Roman Empire. At the same time, a great "sign from heaven" appeared, as Halley's comet also appeared. These two events could have provided the basic idea for a delegation of magi travelling to Bethlehem in response to a great sign.[90]

The story could have been woven together with Isaiah 60:1–6, which tells of foreign people coming to praise the Lord, bringing gold and frankincense. However, in Isaiah, the king also received some camels, but this was not the case with the magi in Bethlehem.

Sceptics who believe that the story is an invention will not be interested in real astronomical events, as this would serve no purpose for them. However, some sceptics still try to connect the story to some real event that might have been a trigger for Christians

---

[90] Jenkins (2004), p. 336; see http://adsabs.harvard.edu/full/2004JBAA..114..336J.

to link it with the birth of Christ. As mentioned above, the appearance of Halley's comet was one such event.

One of the critics of these various theories is Aaron Adair, a physics scholar with an interest in astronomy. His attitude is that for a theory to be true, it needs to explain all of the parts of the story in the Bible. It should explain why the event gave the magi the idea that a king was being born in Israel, why the magi travelled to Israel, and how the star could lead them to Bethlehem and to Christ.[91]

Adair criticises a number of theories, since they all fail to answer all these questions simultaneously. This is a sound attitude. A theory that rests on some real facts and then makes many assumptions to complete the picture is not a very sound theory. In such an approach, the assumptions prove the theory, and assumptions based on nothing are just fantasies.

Adair also maintains that the different interpretations of the sign should point clearly in one direction. If an event could be interpreted in several ways, it is not scientific to say that it must have been interpreted in the way that we prefer. This is also a sound attitude. Our assumptions can never prove a theory.

He addresses a common mistake: people notice something and then leap to the conclusion that it "must be" what the magi saw; the magi's interpretation must have been the same as theirs. Adair is totally correct to point out the futility of interpreting astronomical events in this way. It will be attractive to people who are already convinced, but it will not convince anyone to change their opinion – at least, no critically minded person. The expression "must be" or "must have" is common in texts trying to explain the Star of Bethlehem. But to build an entire case on "must" is actually nothing more than an admission that the theory does not rest on facts, but on guesses.

---

[91] Adair (2013), pp. 15, 114-117.

Adair's approach is good as a methodology, but he is too positivistic in demanding that everyone should reach the same conclusion. A scientific theory is scientific not because it convinces everyone, but because it rests on a sound methodology. Competing theories will exist, and competing theories are more likely to occur in the softer sciences, such as history.

The interpretation of events in the night sky by ancient diviners is not physics; it rests on human imagination and human errors. Adair states that astrology is not scientific, since experiments show that astrologers draw different conclusions from the same data. In saying this, he effectively rules out the possibility of finding a solution to the problem of the Star of Bethlehem. To some degree, this is correct too. If astrology as we know it today were the basis for the diviners, we would not be able to tell how they would have interpreted the sky. However, we have seen that the diviners of Babylon were more mechanical in their interpretations. The number of possible interpretations was limited, if the magi used Enuma Anu Enlil.

Nevertheless, astrology was still being developed in the Greco-Roman world, so there were no consistent rules for how to interpret the night sky. To look at rare celestial events and connect those events to Greco-Roman astrology would therefore inevitably lead to numerous competing theories, which would not be convincing.

If we are able to find an interpretation that has an answer for what the magi saw, why they went to Israel and how the star led them to Bethlehem, this would obviously be a good thing; but since we are dealing with human interpretation, we must accept a situation where some parts of our theory may be less convincing.

This is especially important for sceptics to consider. A sceptic must realise that a good theory rests on several conclusions. In fact, we can compare this to a murder case. Some pieces of evidence will be clearer than others; some will be circumstantial and others will be more directly relevant. All these pieces of evidence must be considered individually, so we can ask: what supports our theory, and what does not support our theory? Not all aspects of a murder can be proved. Sometimes a jury realises that the murderer must have done this or that, even though there is no evidence for that action. This would still be a reasonable conclusion, if there is sufficient hard evidence proving that the murderer has been correctly identified. If this is the case, some assumptions can be made as to what "must have happened", in order to complete the picture.

In the area of religion, people tend to draw conclusions too quickly, and the conclusion tends to be the one that fits with the basic beliefs that the individual already holds. But just as a believer must not hasten to explain away the difficulties, in the same way, the sceptic must not hasten to explain away individual findings. When each piece of evidence has been considered individually, we must weigh up all the evidence collectively and decide in what direction it all seems to point.

The Christian reader is cautioned not to look away from difficult facts, but the non-Christian reader is also cautioned to have an open mind. An open mind is always a sceptical mind, because the most basic scientific approach is for us to be sceptical of ourselves; it is very easy for us to end up seeing what we want to see, rather than what is actually there.

7.2 Candidates for the Star of Bethlehem

We shall now examine the different objects and events that occurred in the night sky at the relevant moment, and assess how good they are as candidates for explaining the Star of Bethlehem.

7.2.1 Comets and meteors

Meteors are poor candidates in the search for the Star of Bethlehem. The reason is that the biblical story clearly says that the magi saw something in the east, which made them travel to Jerusalem; from there, the star led them to Bethlehem. A meteor is only visible for a short while, and it cannot stay in a fixed position in the sky.

Comets, like Halley's comet, are visible for a longer period of time. However, all the evidence available to us makes it clear that a comet would have been seen as a bad omen.[92]

7.2.2 Novae and supernovae

Adair rules out novae and supernovae. The basic reason for this scepticism is that Chinese astronomers were very interested in recording such events, and we have no record of any novae or supernovae at the appropriate time. A theory resting on a nova or supernova would thus not be valid, since we have no reason to believe that such an event occurred at that time.

7.2.3 Planets

Planets are better candidates for being the Star of Bethlehem. The reason for this is that diviners in the Greco-Roman world, as well as in Babylonia, were particularly interested in the movements of the planets. In fact, astrology and divination would not be based on much if the planets had not been there. The movements of the planets create interesting events and rare phenomena, and without them, the night sky would be an almost static scene.

7.2.4 Stars

Stars are poor candidates for the Star of Bethlehem. The reason is that stars stay in the sky where they have always been. If the story of the Star of Bethlehem is based on real events, the reason the magi travelled to Jerusalem could not have been because of a static star.

---

[92] Adair (2013), pp. 31–41.

7.2.5 Constellations

Constellations, like stars, are poor candidates to be the Star of Bethlehem, since they too are static and cannot be interpreted.

7.3 The three main celestial events suggested to be the Star of Bethlehem

Over the ages, people have tried to identify strange or very rare events that occurred in the skies prior to the birth of Christ. In a way, the night sky is like a huge clockwork machine, where some events are common, such as a new moon; some events are rarer, such as an eclipse; and some events are extremely rare, such as three planets coming close to each other. Rare events are thus good candidates for what might have triggered the magi's trip to Jerusalem.

A special form of event is when a planet halts and starts to travel in the opposite direction (retrograde movement). In Chapter 1.5 we saw that the planets regularly reach a stationary point and change direction. As such, this is not very rare, but we also saw in Chapter 2.4 that stationary points were studied and that the magi wrote these down in their diaries when they occurred.

When a planet reaches a stationary point it changes direction, and then some time later, it will reach a second stationary point and change direction again. In Chapter 1.5, we saw that this could be seen as an s-shaped path in the sky, which takes place in one or two star signs, depending on where the planet is when it first reaches a stationary point. Thus, the s-shaped movement could be seen as marking a specific star sign, and this in itself could be seen as a strange phenomenon.

Another strange phenomenon could be a conjunction of planets. As we saw in Chapter 1.6, once in approximately every 800 years Jupiter and Saturn perform a great conjunction. A further unusual event is when two planets or one planet and a star come very close to each other, or even occult each other; that is, one stands in front of the other.

It is possible that an event such as those described above might have been the basis for the story of the Star of Bethlehem.

7.3.1 Conjunction of Jupiter and Saturn in 7 BC

In 7 BC, Jupiter and Saturn performed a conjunction in Pisces (the Fishes), and in the eighth century AD a Jewish Persian astrologer, Masha'allah, suggested that this conjunction could be the Star of Bethlehem. However, he was instead describing the *great conjunction* in 26 BC, which happened in Leo. He probably learnt about great conjunctions from the priests of the Persian religion Zoroastrianism, where great conjunctions were of great importance. However, 26 BC is far too early for our star.

The Zoroastrians knew that great conjunctions happened in different areas of the sky, which are called *trines*, but this theory was developed several hundred years after the birth of Christ, as we saw in Chapter 1.6. Completely damaging to this theory is the fact that Zoroastrians were originally uninterested in stars and divination. They only began to practice divination in the third century AD, so the whole basis for this theory vanishes[93] (see Chapter 8).

The next attempt to explain the Star of Bethlehem was the conjunction of 7 BC. A Muslim astrologer, Abu Ma'shar, suggested this in the eighth century AD, and the idea was later adopted by Kepler. This conjunction happened in Pisces, as noted above.[94]

According to this theory, Saturn and Pisces are connected to the Jews, while Jupiter was linked to kingship. Thus, the magi would have interpreted this as a sign that a great king would be born to the

---

[93] Adair (2013), p. 110.
[94] Adair (2013), pp. 65–68.

Jews. Adair questions this, and says there is no proof that either Saturn or Pisces were ever connected to the Jewish people.[95]

However, the theory about the conjunction in 7 BC has also been put forward by an Assyriologist, Simo Parpola. Strangely enough, he does not refer to the Babylonian divination manual, Enuma Anu Enlil. Instead, he refers to the Persian view of great conjunctions, which he asserts had no meaning in Babylonian divination. He points out that Mars joined the conjunction. Mars is connected to Amurru in Babylonian divination, and Amurru is a second millennium BC name for the area from present-day Israel to Syria. Parpola suggests that the involvement of Mars was the sign that made the magi go to King Herod, as he was the important king of the area.[96]

As we can see, Parpola's interpretation is anachronistic, since it is based on the concept of great conjunctions, which was not recorded until centuries later.

7.3.2 Jupiter retrograding above Regulus in 3 BC and 2 BC

Jupiter regularly passes Regulus, which is the brightest star in Leo. It takes approximately twelve years for Jupiter to complete its journey around the sun, and thus Jupiter passes Regulus at least once every twelve years. However, the passing over Regulus can sometimes coincide with a retrograde motion. In such cases, Jupiter will pass Regulus three times in less than a year.

Since Jupiter represents the highest god in Rome as well as in Babylonia, it is the principal planet and represents kingship.

The name Regulus means "prince" or "little king". One theory is that the triple meeting in 3 BC and 2 BC was interpreted as a sign that the gods had chosen a new king, or more precisely, that a new

---

[95] Adair (2013), pp. 65–68.
[96] Parpola (2009), pp. 13–24.

king would be born. Since the sign occurred in the Lion, and Israel/Judah was seen as being connected to the Lion, some think that this was an omen about an important Jewish prince being born.[97]

In reality, the Babylonians did not have an omen for the complete s-shaped movement above Regulus. Such long events were not of interest in their divination manual. An interesting event for them would have been if Jupiter had passed Regulus and then moved in retrograde out of the breast of Leo:

> And the matter of the planet Jupiter is as follows: If it turns back out of the Breast of Leo, this is ominous. It is written in the Series as follows: "If Jupiter passes Regulus and gets ahead of it, and afterward Regulus, which it passed and got ahead of, stays within its setting, someone will rise, kill the king and seize the throne." This aforesaid is the only area which is taken as bad if Jupiter retrogrades there. Wherever else it might turn, it may freely do so, there is not a word about it.[98]

In other words, the retrograde movement of Jupiter above Regulus was a known phenomenon to the magi, and they knew how to interpret it. It had nothing to do with the birth of a king, and it had nothing to do with Israel. The omen always happened in Leo, and they did not consider Leo to represent Israel. The prediction was, rather, that the king of Akkad would die and the dynasty would change. We have every reason to believe the magi studied it. The reason we can say this with confidence is that the magi took notes regarding the date when the planet passed normal stars (as we saw in Chapter 2.4), and Regulus is one of the normal stars. Given the graveness of the omen, it would probably have been of great interest to the magi.

---

[97] Larson (2017).
[98] Rochberg (2010), p. 377.

7.3.3 Conjunction of Jupiter and Venus on 17th June 2 BC

Jupiter and Venus came close to each other on several occasions in the year 2 BC, and on 17th June that year the two planets came so close to each other that to the naked eye it looked as if they had merged into a new star. The brightest objects in the sky are the sun, the moon, Venus and Jupiter. When Venus and Jupiter come right next to each other, their joint light is considerably stronger, seeming like a very bright star or planet. Such a conjunction is very rare and would have been of great interest to the magi, especially since it is mentioned in Enuma Anu Enlil.

Since Venus represents fertility in Rome as well as in Babylonia, and since Jupiter represents kingship, some argue that their merging was interpreted as the birth of a new king.[99] In reality, the interpretation was quite different, and this depended on how close the two planets came together. Thus, the magi would have been eager to study their approach for a couple of days to see how close these planets would come to each other. The closer they came, the more predictions there would be, in the following order:

- There will be a flood.
- Brother will be hostile to brother.
- There will be a rule of destruction (concerning) the king of Amurru.
- The king of Akkad will die and the dynasty will change, and either the enemy will send a messenger or a soldier will be sent to the enemy asking for peace.[100]

The conjunction took place in the west, a direction called *Amurru*. This is the name in the divination manual for present-day Israel, Lebanon, Jordan and western Syria. If the omen did not specify

---

[99] Larson (2017).
[100] Reiner and Pingree (1998), p. 45.

which geographical area the omen concerned, the place in the sky where the event took place could be seen as an indication as to where the omen would take effect. However, this was not the normal way to interpret these particular signs; the normal way would have identified that they concerned Akkad, as we saw earlier.

The theory that the conjunction of Jupiter and Venus directed the magi to Jerusalem because it happened in the west is therefore not as clear as it seems. However, our uncertainty can be settled by Enuma Anu Enlil. According to the divination manual the meeting of Venus and Jupiter also meant that there would be a "reign of destruction (concerning) the king of Amurru"[101] (see Chapter 7.6.6). That the sign happened in the west would thus not be the primary reason for the magi to travel to Jerusalem; but it would strengthen their assumption that Amurru was involved in the coming of a new king.

However, this sign in no way would have meant that a prince would be born, either in Akkad or in Judah. It is just fantasy to see this as a sign of birth. We have no evidence that a merging of Jupiter and Venus would have been seen as heralding any birth, let alone the birth of a king.

7.3.4 Combination of events in 3 BC and 2 BC

Some argue that the events in 3 BC and 2 BC were interpreted as one great sign by the magi. Larson argues that the magi noticed how Jupiter marked Regulus in early September in 3 BC, and took it as a sign that a prince would be born. The conjunction of Jupiter and Venus on 17th June in 2 BC, according to Larson, was then seen as confirmation that the prince had been born. The two events were nine months (39.7 weeks) apart, which the magi would have noticed.[102] Important to Larson, is that the sign was observed in the morning of the new Jewish month, which is also the Jewish New

---

[101] Reiner and Pingree (1998), p. 45.
[102] Larson (2017).

Year. This would be the 11th of September. However, the most interesting day to the magi would be the 13th, when Jupiter enters Leo.

As we saw above, none of these events would have been interpreted as the birth of a prince. However, the theory is interesting. Both events could have been seen as omens that the king would die and the dynasty would change. At that time, Mesopotamia was occupied by the Parthian Empire, which had its base in Persia. The king was, in other words, an occupying force, and we know that the Babylonian population were not happy with the state of affairs. They had revolted on several occasions, and in a few decades, they would try to evict the occupiers again.

An omen suggesting that the king of Akkad would die would thus be seen as a good omen, especially in the city of Babylon, which had been very harshly treated for centuries. Babylon was slowly turning into a city of ruins, and the religion of its main temples was under threat from other foreign religions (see Chapter 4.5).

If the magi saw the connection between the two events, they might have concluded that a king of Judah (given the lack of other important kings in the Amurru area) would overthrow the king of Akkad. Since the other sign came nine months after the first, it is possible to suppose that the magi might have seen this as a sign that the king had been born, but this is just an assumption.

The political situation of the time and the interpretation of the signs according to Enuma Anu Enlil make it fully possible that the magi would consider a trip to Jerusalem, especially since the divination manual also suggested that a soldier would be sent to the enemy (see Chapter 7.3.3). Without a soldier at hand, the magi might have been tempted to travel to Israel to proclaim what they had seen, in order to strengthen the possibility that the omen would come true.

To us it might seem unrealistic that a Jewish king would reach such importance at that time; however, the magi of Babylon would probably have thought of Alexander the Great, who had managed to crush the mighty Persian Empire despite his origins as just the king of a small part of Greece (see Chapter 4.5).

7.3.5 The trip from Jerusalem to Bethlehem

The theories above only try to explain why the magi came to believe that a prince had been born in Israel. As we have seen, none of the events actually directly predicted the birth of a prince. However, we saw that the signs could very well have triggered a trip to see the new king. But nothing has so far been said about Bethlehem, so what was the sign that directed them there?

Some people who try to explain the Star of Bethlehem do not try to explain everything. They might consider it pure fiction that the star went before the magi from Jerusalem to Bethlehem.

Those who try to explain this final stage often stress that when a planet changes direction it will appear to slow down and, for a while, appear to stand still. Larson, to take one example, says that the magi travelled to Bethlehem on 25th December, when Jupiter stopped. When they left King Herod, they would have seen Jupiter in the south (in the direction of Bethlehem), and it would have been in the south while the magi took the short trip of perhaps eight kilometres between Jerusalem and Bethlehem. As they arrived in Bethlehem, the planet would have reached its stationary point and then remained fixed in the night sky.[103]

To Adair, this explanation is not plausible. The slowing down of a planet as it changes direction is such a slow process that the exact point at which it stands still is not observable. He suggests that the planet actually appears to be standing still for days – so Jupiter would have appeared to be standing still in Jerusalem as well as in

---

[103] Larson (2017).

Bethlehem. It would not have changed position during the short trip between the two.[104]

When Adair wrote this, he was not aware that the magi could actually calculate the speed of Jupiter; that they could do so has only just been discovered, in 2016.[105] However, their calculation would only have given a rough speed, and could not have been used to decide the exact moment in time when the star stood still.

Adair makes another good point: the idea of the magi moving freely around the countryside following a star does not take into consideration the fact that the area was inhabited by farmers, or that it had high hills and steep areas. Furthermore, Jupiter – if this was the Star of Bethlehem – was not seen in the early evenings in December in 2 BC. It rose very late, at roughly 9 pm. If the magi travelled that late, their journey would have been made over tricky terrain in complete darkness (there would have been no light from the moon), and if they had gone past (or even to) any of the houses, the inhabitants would probably have been asleep and likely to have thought them to be robbers or intruders.

A more realistic view (if Jupiter was the Star of Bethlehem) is that the magi travelled early in the morning, when Jupiter was still visible. This is in practice what Larson suggests. In the early morning, Jupiter was south of Jerusalem, and thus in the direction of Bethlehem.

If the magi travelled in the early morning they would probably have followed the normal route between Jerusalem and Bethlehem: Derech Beit Lechem. This route follows the terrain and slowly turns to the west. If the magi started at a suitable hour, they would have had Jupiter in front of them as they left Jerusalem. If they travelled by donkey, camel or horse – slightly faster than the speed of walking

---

[104] Adair (2013), p. 57.
[105] See http://phys.org/news/2016-01-babylonian-astronomers-position-jupiter-geometric.html, (read 2016-12-04)

– they would have had Jupiter in front of them all the way to Bethlehem, since Jupiter would have moved slowly to the west just as the road slowly turned west.

When the magi approached Bethlehem, which at that time was probably a very tiny settlement, Jupiter might have appeared to rest on top of a house, which the magi went into. Such a journey could, thus, be seen by the magi as if Jupiter had gone before them all the way to Bethlehem, and finally stopped over the right house.

Adair would perhaps disagree, and say that Jupiter never stopped above the house, as the Bible says. However, Adair does not sufficiently examine the diviners and their beliefs. As we saw in Chapter 2.4, the magi did study when the planets reached their stationary point, that is, when they made a halt. In fact, that was one of the main things the magi studied (see Chapter 2.4).

Adair's mistake is that to him, a halt is a speed of exactly zero metres per second – that is, no movement at all. This is a halt in the modern mind, but the magi did not have such precision. They used their fingers to study the movements of planets, and when they could not measure a movement (because it was moving so slowly), they reached the conclusion that the planet had halted. From a modern scientific point of view, the magi were not able to tell exactly when the planet stopped. However, this is not important; what matters is that the magi had some sort of rule for telling when the planet stopped, and they had used this rule for centuries as they recorded the stationary points on a regular basis. Adair's line of reasoning thus misses the point completely.

As we saw above, it is likely that the magi travelled in the morning, if they went to Judah in 2 BC. It is thus quite possible that they found that Jupiter had stopped in the morning. Such an event is actually described in Enuma Anu Enlil.

Given the fact that most omens were bad, the probability of a bad omen was very high; but even higher was the probability that the omen predicted something that was nothing to do with the search for a new king: perhaps Jupiter standing still meant that a disease would come, or that lions would kill many cattle. But in fact, it turned out that the omen was actually very fitting:

> If Jupiter becomes steady in the morning, enemy kings will be reconciled.[106]

Since the Akkadian words for "reconciliation" and "peace" are the same, the sign over Bethlehem could have been interpreted as a peace sign. However, the Bible does not say whether or how the magi interpreted this sign. Matthew only says:

> 9 When they heard the king, they departed. And the star which they saw in the east went before them until it came and stood over where the young Child was. 10 When they saw the star, they rejoiced with great excitement.[107]

Could it be that they became glad when they saw the heavens proclaiming that their new king would be a Prince of Peace, as God had already told the Jews?[108] If the magi had some sort of written document describing what they had predicted, this last event, as they arrived in Bethlehem, might not have been included; and this could explain why nothing is said in the Bible about what it meant when the star stood still.

The omen series suggested that a soldier should be sent asking for peace. Maybe this suggestion gave them the idea to travel. It they saw the star of peace as they arrived – no wonder they rejoiced with great excitement!

---

[106] Reiner and Pingree (1998), p. 224.
[107] The Bible (MEV), Matthew 2:9–10.
[108] The Bible (MEV), Isaiah 9:6.

7.4 Could a single planet be a sufficient sign?

The Star of Bethlehem is a single star, according to the Bible. A critical reader will notice that the explanations above include other stars or planets. The theories tend to describe the Star of Bethlehem as a single star when it is suitable, and as many stars or planets in other cases.[109] This is a valid objection.

However, in Akkadian times, in the Greco-Roman world and even in the modern era, the word "star" has both the narrow meaning that we have, and a wider meaning of *sign*. Thus, a star could be a single star or planet, a constellation, or the message conveyed by such. This goes all the way back to Sumerian times, when the symbol for "star" could also be used for *constellation*, or even a character in a text (see Chapter 2.3). A cuneiform letter is thus seen as a sign.

Therefore, when the magi say that they have seen a star, this does not exclude the possibility that they have actually seen this star in relation to another star (or planet). The typical omen is a planet in relation to another planet or star. This is not the same as saying that there were several Stars of Bethlehem. The basic planet in all of the signs mentioned above is Jupiter. The involvement of Jupiter is not necessary for an omen to be about kingship, but Jupiter is the king star, and the involvement of Jupiter often turns an omen into an omen about kingship.

Thus, from the perspective of Enuma Anu Enlil, Jupiter is the king star, and the movement of Jupiter would tell the magi about the present or coming king. If the magi referred to a planet in the singular, they would most likely have thought about Jupiter. However, as mentioned above, they used the word "star" in a more general sense. When they said that they had seen the child's star, they would also have thought of and intended the omens they saw. As outlined above, a planet in itself conveys no meaning, but planets

---

[109] Münter (1827), pp. 19–21.

are the main agents (through their movements) in interpreting the sky, alongside the moon to some extent.

7.5 Are we ready to draw a conclusion?

We have seen that Persian astrologers did not exist at the time of the birth of Christ. We have seen that the divination manual in Babylon does not tell us about the birth of a king, at least not based on the signs we have studied. Adair would, rightly, argue that we have in no way found any evidence to support the fact that the magi travelled to Jerusalem to meet a newborn king.

However, we are not yet ready to draw a conclusion. The divination manual seems to have been neglected in the study of the Star of Bethlehem thus far. Without the divination manual, the events we have studied have simply been chosen by modern people according to modern thinking, which at best uses the Greco-Roman view of stars and planets.

However, in our study we have seen that these modern interpretations have neglected Enuma Anu Enlil. Due to this, the events in the night sky have not been interpreted in the way the magi would have interpreted them. The magi did not only study strange phenomena. They studied many things, and events that seem unimportant to us might have been important to them. We must take a closer look at Enuma Anu Enlil, as there might be other events, not previously mentioned or noticed, that make the picture complete.

Larson has suggested that Revelation 12 is a description of what the magi saw,[110] and we will now examine if his theory is valid. We shall do so by comparing the text of Revelation 12 with the divination manual. After that, we will be ready for a conclusion.

---

[110] Larson (2017).

7.6 Is the sign about a New Alexander the Great?

In the rest of the chapter, we will see that it is very likely that Larson is correct in his assumption that Revelation 12 reflects what the magi saw. However, the signs would not have been interpreted in the way he suggests. The magi's interpretation would have been from their own point of view, using their manual and their religion to try to understand the message in the sky.

The theory in this book is that what the magi saw in the sky were signs telling them about the birth of a new Alexander the Great figure, who would overthrow the king of Akkad and restore Babylon to power. A Christian reader might find this strange, but we must remember that the Bible does not say that the magi believed in God. They only came to visit the newborn king; what they thought of him is not mentioned anywhere in the Bible.

7.6.1 What we see in the stars

On 13th September 3 BC, the year of the Star of Bethlehem, the new moon appeared in the west. To the Babylonians, as well as to the Jews, this heralded the start of a new month. To the Jews, it was also the start of a New Year. Today the Jewish calendar is more regular, but at that time the actual sighting was important. We cannot say for certain that the moon was seen on the 13th – it might have been seen on the 12th or the 14th, but this does not matter for our study.

To the Babylonians it was important to study the new moon on the morning of the new month (see Chapter 2.4). On this day, and on several days to follow, the moon would not have been visible above the horizon at daybreak. Thus, we do not know with certainty that they got up early in the morning to look at the night sky.

However, the mornings of the 13th and 14th were special in another way: Jupiter passed Regulus in the Lion, and came very close to it.

At daybreak on these days, the moon would have been at the feet of Virgo. The sun would then have lit up Virgo, and this would have told the magi that it was the ruling constellation among the star signs at that moment. On these two dates, Jupiter would also have been at its closest to Regulus, and when they saw this, the magi would have known that it was a sign of the death of the king of Akkad; it would have been the first time they witnessed this in their lifetimes. As was mentioned above, the magi would have been recording the time when Jupiter passed Regulus, so we have every reason to believe they were out observing the sky on these mornings.

7.6.2 The crowned woman clothed with the sun

According to Revelation, a great sign appeared in heaven. A woman clothed with the sun with twelve stars on her head was about to give birth.

> A great sign appeared in heaven: a woman clothed with the sun, with the moon under her feet and a crown of twelve stars on her head. 2 She was pregnant and cried out in pain as she was about to give birth.

If we look at the stars' positions, we can see that Virgo is often "clothed with the sun" with the moon at her feet, as it happens every year. We cannot be sure that the author of Revelation meant the woman to be the constellation of Virgo, but if this is the case, we have to take into account that Virgo has the moon at her feet every autumn.

Does she have twelve stars on her head? According to Larson, the twelve stars are the nine main stars of the Lion's asterism, plus Venus, Jupiter and Mars.[111] However, we have seen that the Lion had a different asterism in Babylonia. Hutchinson correctly noticed that the stars of the Lion are not the same today as they were to the Babylonians. He refers to "the research done by several people" that

---

[111] Larson (2017).

make it "possible to establish the western and the eastern boundaries of Leo". Unfortunately, he does not outline who these people are, what their sources were and what stars they included.

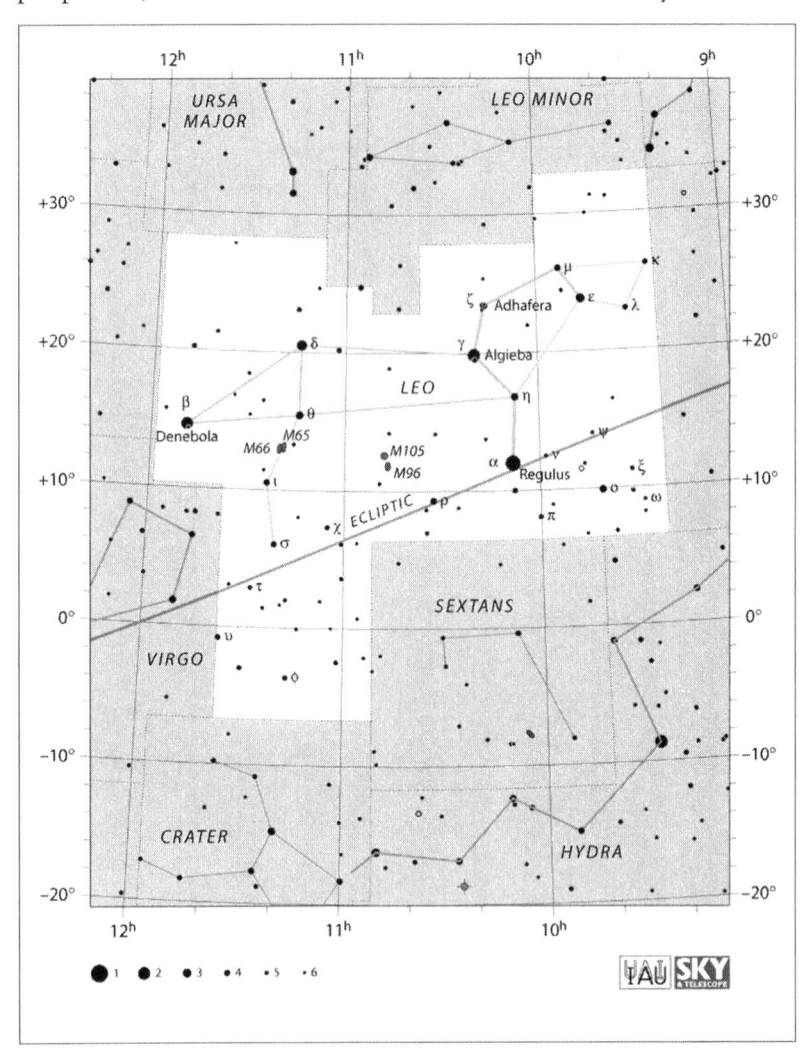

Figure 13. Leo according to the International Astronomical Union

The pattern found on the International Astronomical Union's website is not correct either; it has thirteen stars, and Regulus is one of the feet (see Figure 13). This contradicts Babylonian sources, where Regulus is never said to be one of the feet. Further, the Arabic name for Regulus means "the heart of the Lion".

If the description in Revelation comes from Babylon, Larson can not be right in his assumption about the nine stars plus three planets. The reason is that the Babylonian sources mention the feet of the Lion, while Larson's nine stars do not include any feet at all!

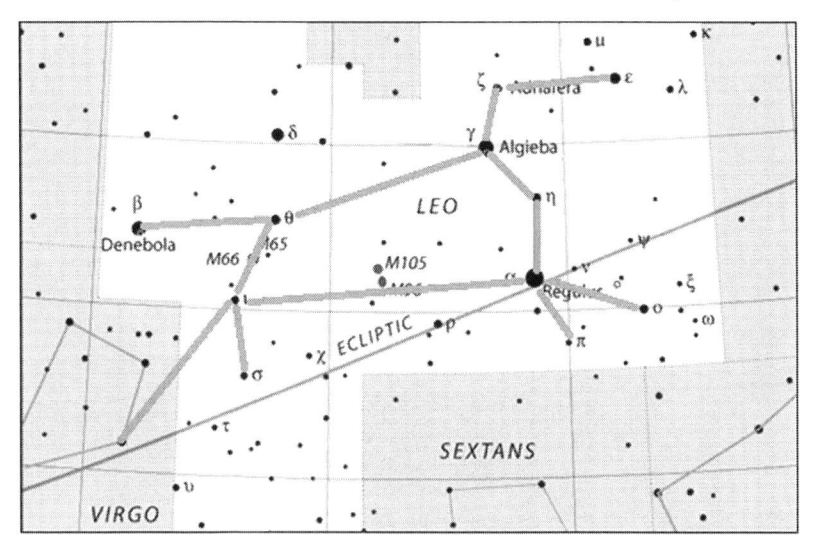

Figure 14. The Lion, in the suggested asterism in this book

However, in Chapter 1.2 we saw that the constellations were altered in Roman times, and an alternative version of the Lion was devised. In this version, the Lion is made up of twelve stars, and sits above the Virgin's head (see Figure 14).

This asterism and the ancient sources do not prove that the Lion was represented with twelve stars. The picture has been made from several sources, but since these are distant in time, we cannot rule out the possibility that the Lion had different representations in different centuries and places. However, the Lion seems to have been seen as a lion on four legs by many cultures in the area.

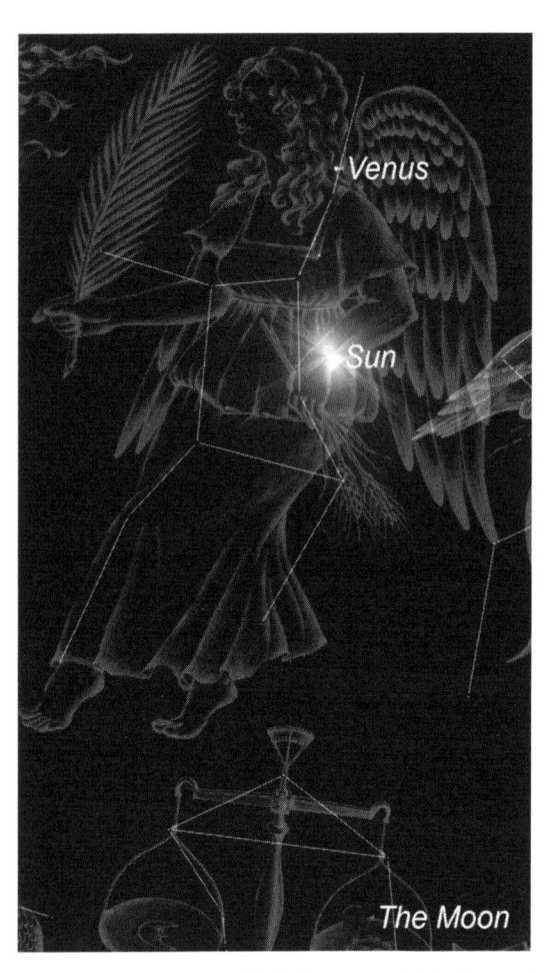

Figure 15. Sunrise in Babylonia on 13th September 3 BC. The horizon has been removed in the figure to display the moon (on Libra, bottom right). [112]

It is therefore possible to see Revelation 12 as a description of the Virgin with the Lion above her head, being lit up by the sun while she had the moon at her feet. However, it is not possible to say for certain that this description ultimately came from Babylonia.

---

[112] Image created with Starry Night software; see https://starrynight.com.

7.6.3 The pregnant woman

Thus far, we have seen that the woman has a crown on her head and the moon at her feet, and she is clothed with the sun – but is she pregnant?

The divination manual does not contain any signs that point to a woman being pregnant. However, there is a sign predicting how easily children will be born. This sign is relevant when Venus has risen before the sun, and is dimmed by the light of the rising sun. This phenomenon was seen at the same time that Jupiter was closest to Regulus, that is, around 13th September 3 BC.

If Venus has the sun at her left side, children will be born with ease. On the mornings in question, Venus had the sun slightly to her right, which is a sign that children will be born with difficulty (see Figure 15).

> If Venus is dimmed at her right side: women will have difficulty giving birth. If Venus is dimmed at her left side: women will have easy childbirth.[113]

In other words, the magi might have combined the information about the birth with the information about the future king, and thus they might have seen this as a prediction that the king was going to be born. If this was combined with the events in the summer of 2 BC, they would perhaps have seen that as the date that the baby would be born, and they might have assumed that he would be a prince of Amurru, or in fact, a Jewish prince.

That the child should be born with great difficulty fits well with the description in Revelation 12:2:

> … καὶ ἐν γαστρὶ ἔχουσα, καὶ κράζει ὠδίνουσα καὶ βασανιζομένη τεκεῖν

---

[113] Reiner and Pingree (1998), p. 93.

A literal translation of this verse is:

> ... and having in womb. And she cries out, being in travail, and being in pain to bring forth.[114]

The sentence above has been translated from Greek in many different ways. The reason is that the Greek words used do not have suitable English translations. John the Presbyter has used two words for the pain of childbirth, and these two words need to be related to the process of giving birth in such a way that the result is an understandable English description. To a Greek reader, the pain is stressed, and the second word used for "pain" is actually related to the word meaning "torture". Thus, it is quite clear that John the Presbyter seems to stress the pain – and this is, as we have seen, in full accordance with the divination manual.

In a personal communication with Dwight Hutchinson[115] in June 2017, he argues that the sun often dims Venus, and thus the dimming refers to another phenomenon. Let us study the omen better! What could dim Venus? The manual is aware that the brightness of Venus is not the same all the time. The reason for this is that Venus actually has phases, just like the moon. This was discovered by Galileo using a telescope. Very rarely, Mercury covers Venus, but in such an observation, the two planets must be visible. According to the terminology in the manual, such an event would be described: "Venus enters behind Mercury". So the event would neither be observed with the naked eye nor described as a dimming. The remaining explanations are the sun, some cloud or that the omen is simply not observable. There are omens for the moon being behind Jupiter, so some omens are clearly impossible. If the magi wanted to make sense of the omen, they could have seen it as a cloud or a dimming by the sun. We can never prove or disprove a dimming of a cloud, but a dimming of the sun is possible to

---

[114] The Bible (Berean), Revelation 12:2.
[115] Author of "The Lion Lead the way", see Hutchinson(2015)

demonstrate. In the manual, Venus is the only "woman" who can and does tell about difficulties giving birth. The omen by itself can not serve as a proof of a Babylonian background to Revelation 12. If we have other reasons to believe that the woman is Venus and if we have sufficient other reasons to believe in the Babylonian background to Revelation 12, the omen about Venus being dimmed ought to be seen as the background to Revelation 12:2.

7.6.4 The birth and the red crowned dragon/serpent

Figure 16. Mushmahhu, the seven-headed dragon with horns [116]

In Revelation 12:3, a seven-headed dragon is introduced as the adversary of the woman and her child.

> 3 Then another sign appeared in heaven: There was a great red dragon with seven heads and ten horns, and seven diadems on his heads. 4 His tail drew a third of the stars of heaven, and threw them to the earth.[117]

---

[116] © Oriental Institute of the University of Chicago; used with permission.
[117] The Bible (MEV), Revelation 12:3–4.

There is a Babylonian dragon/serpent with seven heads called Mushmahhu, which was slain by Ninurta. The dragon is pictured as having strange horns on its back (see Figure 16). There is at least one other image of the dragon, where it also seems to have horns,[118] and while the number of horns differ, in both cases they are on the back rather than on the head.

As we saw above (see Chapter 5.2), the stories about Ninurta influenced the stories about Hercules – in this case, his killing of the Lernean Hydra. While the Hydra is thought to have had nine heads, seven heads and other numbers of heads have also been mentioned in various sources.

The Babylonian dragon story is actually about five thousand years old, but it must have survived up to the first millennium BC in order to be transmitted to the Greeks. The Babylonian magi are known to have valued ancient texts and preserved them. The Babylonian priest Berossos, for instance, knew and preferred the Sumerian creation myth (see Chapter 5.1). Since Nabu had become the main war god, he (or Mercury) would have been regarded as the dragon killer.

Neither the Hydra nor Mushmahhu were red, nor had a crown or diadem,[119] as in the above description in Revelation 12:3. However, a Babylonian magus would have recognised this description as being a reference to Mercury, which had the power to "crown" something beneath it and colour it red. According to Babylonian divination theory, the planets gave their colour to the objects they passed over. The passing in itself was said to put a crown or diadem on the object.[120] It is thus clear that the crowning and colouring are connected to planets coming near to other planets. A crown can, for instance, be red, or the planet as such can become red, and it

---

[118] Image in custody of Bible Lands Museum, Israel.
[119] Theoi Greek Mythology; see
http://www.theoi.com/Ther/DrakonHydra.html.
[120] Reiner and Pingree (1998), pp. 23, 59, 126, 181.

signifies the presence of Mercury or Mars above the object becoming red and crowned.

Figure 17. Mercury above the seven-headed dragon (to the right of the Lion's front foot). [121]

On 17th June 2 BC, Mercury was above the head of the dragon (the Hydra) in prograde motion, but some forty days later it stood still and went into retrograde motion, still over the head of the dragon. A magus hearing that the seven-headed dragon was red and crowned would expect to see exactly this in the sky!

7.6.5 The fight between the archangel Michael and the dragon

When the child was born, there was a fight between the archangel Michael and the dragon:

> 7 Then war broke out in heaven. Michael and his angels fought against the dragon, and the dragon and his angels fought, 8 but they did not prevail, nor was there a place for them in heaven any longer. 9 The great dragon was cast out, that ancient serpent called the

---

[121] Image created with Starry Night software; see https://starrynight.com.

Devil and Satan, who deceives the whole world. He was cast down to the earth, and his angels were cast down with him.[122]

If we had looked at the night sky in the summer of the year 2 BC, we would have seen that Mercury was in retrograde above the head of the seven-headed dragon, which we today call the Hydra.

During this event, the dragon fell under the horizon and was finally no longer seen in the sky. The tail would have been the last part of the Hydra to be seen above the horizon.

As we have seen, Mercury is Nabu – in effect, the principal active god in Babylon at that time. In Chapter 6 we saw that he was represented by an angel-like figure, according to both Ezekiel and Babylonian temple art. We also know that angels and planets were thought to be connected. Thus, it is fully possible to imagine that those reading the sky at the time saw a fight between an angel and dragon taking place that summer, and it is also possible that they saw how the angel fought the dragon down to earth.

Each summer the Hydra falls to earth, and in August, when the Hydra has fallen, we see the Perseid meteor shower, which could be what Revelation 12 means by angels being thrown down to earth together with the dragon.

In other words, the event of the Hydra falling to earth would have been visible to the magi every year. Every year Mercury comes close to the Hydra as it approaches the setting sun, because Mercury is always close to the sun. However, Mercury can only be seen faintly in the night sky, and often cannot be seen at all due to being so close to the sun or sometimes below the sun.

In the year 2 BC, however, Mercury was high above the sun, and it would have been visible for some time after sunset. This does not happen every year – only roughly one year out of every three – but

---

[122] The Bible (MEV), Revelation 12:7–9.

to the magi, this would still have been a reoccurring phenomenon. Although there is no proof that they saw this as a fight between Nabu/Mercury and the dragon, the description in Revelation fits with what could be seen in the night sky.

7.6.6 Conclusion about the woman and the fight

The omens relevant for 13th September 3 BC were:

- Someone will rise, kill the king and seize the throne.[123]
- Women will have difficulty giving birth.[124]

The omens relevant for 17th June 2 BC were:

> If Venus reaches Sulpae [another name for Jupiter] and they follow upon each other: high water will carry off the land. If Venus reaches ditto and passes it: a mighty high water will come. If Venus and ditto come close: reign of destruction (concerning) the king of Amurru. If Venus comes near ditto: the land altogether – brother will become hostile to his brother. If Venus enters Jupiter (UD.AL.Tar): the king of Akkad will die, the dynasty will change, either a soldier will go out or the enemy will send a message (asking for peace) to the land.[125]

In the omens above, we can see that the closer Venus comes to Jupiter, the worse this is for Akkad and the king of Akkad. The signs in 3 BC and 2 BC both meant that the king of Akkad would die and the dynasty would change; these signs were nine months apart. The destruction would come from Amurru, and the sign was seen to the west, in the direction of Amurru.

---

[123] Rochberg (2010), p. 377.
[124] Reiner and Pingree (1998), p. 93.
[125] Reiner and Pingree (1998), p. 45.

It is very probable, then, that the magi would have connected these two signs. There would be a war with Amurru; the king from Amurru would kill the king of Akkad and take the throne. The sign about a difficult pregnancy, plus the time span of nine months between the two, could then have been interpreted as a sign that the new king was about to be born, in a difficult birth. Thus, the description in Revelation 12 fits perfectly with the omens.

Since Babylon was occupied by Parthia and in a bad state, we can understand why the omens were interesting to the magi. They would probably have hoped that the new king would become another Alexander the Great who would kill the king of Parthia, and in heaven this fight was represented by Nabu fighting the dragon. To the magi, the dragon would have represented the king of Parthia. However, although the skies showed them what the gods' plans were, the gods could change their plans. To travel with a delegation to a king of Amurru would thus have been a good idea, especially since such a delegation is described in the omen: "either a soldier will go out or the enemy will send a message (asking for peace) to the land".

Since the Venus omens identified the enemy as coming from Amurru, we have the basis for the magi's travel to Jerusalem; and when they arrived in Bethlehem, they saw Jupiter at its standstill position in the morning, and thus received the message that the kings would be reconciled (see Chapter 7.3.5). From the magi's point of view, the omens were perfect! They came to Christ hoping that he would be the solution to their problems, in the same way as people have always done to suit their own needs and ideas.

7.6.7 The woman and her hiding place
The dragon was after the woman during her pregnancy, and then pursued both her and the child after the birth. When the child was born, the woman fled:

5 She gave birth to a male Child, "who was to rule all nations with an iron scepter." And her Child was caught up to God and to His throne. 6 The woman fled into the wilderness where she has a place prepared by God, that they may nourish her there for one thousand two hundred and sixty days.[126]

The woman in the summer of 2 BC is Venus, sometimes known as the Queen of Heaven – that is, a combination of the Virgin and Venus. As the Virgin, she is called Ninhursag, and is the mother of Ninurta.

In Enuma Anu Enlil, Venus and the other planets are known to have "secret places", also called "secret houses". Scholars have tried to connect the Babylonian concept of a *secret place* with the Greek idea of an *exaltation*. Both terms seem to mean a place in the sky that is favourable for the planet, where it gains in strength. This idea fits well with the text in Revelation, where the woman seeks nourishment.

However, it is difficult to harmonise the secret places in Babylonia with the Greek exaltations; the former seems to be a constellation, while the latter is expressed as a longitude.[127] In addition, the longitudes used in Greece differ from the known Babylonian secret places. The secret place of Venus is difficult to locate if we try to find it only with the help of Enuma Anu Enlil.[128] There is only one text that can help us locate the secret place of Venus, and that is a horoscope from the third century BC; in this case, Venus is in Scorpio, so this is the only place that has evidence to support it being the secret place.

This location is not a matter of a modern interpretation. The text describes where different planets are and clearly says that "Venus

---

[126] The Bible (MEV), Revelation 12:5–6.
[127] Rochberg (1998), pp. 46–50.
[128] Hunger and Pingree (1999), p. 28.

[is] in Scorpius". The text concludes with: "In the *bit nisirti* of Venus, the child was born."¹²⁹ *Bit nisirti* has the same meaning as *secret place*. Actually, all known texts where a planet is said to be in its secret house or place, places the planet in Scorpio or Libra, which does not fit at all with the Greek exaltations.

Since the evidence is scarce, however, it is difficult to say with certainty where the secret place of Venus is, and having only one source of reference is not much. Scholars try to solve this by connecting the secret places with the Greek exaltations, in order to perhaps find a better foundation for the theory; but in doing so they neglect the single clear reference in the hope of finding a better solution.

If we look at the position of Venus on 17th June 2 BC and then study her continued path, we can see that 1,260 days after the child was born, Venus does indeed appear in Scorpio. If Scorpio is accepted as the secret place, the story fits perfectly with the events in the sky.

Venus passes Scorpio every year, at least once and often twice. So why should Venus run to her secret place and seek nourishment there in 1,260 days? In fact, what matters in Enuma Anu Enlil is how she reaches her secret place:

> If Venus becomes visible in the West and reaches her secret place and disappears: the gods will be reconciled with Amurru.¹³⁰

Venus becoming visible in the west means that she is seen as an evening star. Venus is always close to the sun in the sky, since her path is close to the sun. If she is seen in the west, it is thus in relation with the setting sun.

---

[129] Rochberg (1998), pp.77–78.
[130] Reiner and Pingree (1998), p. 252.

What the omen describes is that Venus is first seen as an evening star, then she approaches and reaches her secret place, and finally disappears.

This pattern was seen in the autumn of AD 2, for the first time since June 2 BC. In September she reached her secret place, and in late October she went under the horizon. During these months, she went into retrograde motion, so she stayed in Scorpio for a long time. On 24th November AD 2 (1,255 days after 17th June 2 BC) she reached her secondary stationary point; that is, she stopped for the second time, and turned to prograde motion. Five days later, she had completed her c-shaped turn, and continued in prograde motion heading out of Scorpio.

It is not possible to say exactly where the borders of Scorpio are, and to the Babylonians a constellation does not actually have borders; it is an asterism, rather than an area of the sky, as it is today. Since there is no clear border, it would be difficult to specify the exact day when Venus left Scorpio.

The interesting thing is not when she left Scorpio anyway, but what she did there: she hid and sought nourishment. The interesting day is thus when she, so to speak, decided to leave the hiding place. This happened on approximately the 1,260th day; she stood still on the 1,255th day and then sped up, and headed out of Scorpio.

The omen suggests that this means that the gods were reconciled with Amurru; that is, the gods brought peace – and ultimately, victory – to Amurru. Which day would be the day of victory? It could not be the last day Venus entered Scorpio to hide, or either of the two stationary points, since being stationary is equivalent to being in hiding. The victory day would probably be a date after the 1,255th day, and to pick the 1,260th day is to pick the date when Venus clearly decided to come out of hiding.

A critical reader might look up the position of Venus on 25th November (the 1,255th day) and say that Venus is in Libra on this day. This is true if we look at how the asterisms look today. However, to the Babylonians, Scorpio's claws reached around Libra.[131] A text from 7 BC tells us that the border between Scorpio and Libra was inside our current Libra[132], so Venus is indeed in Scorpio at this time, between the ancient arms of Scorpio. This area has no visible stars, and fits well with Revelation 12:6, where the woman is said to be in the ἔρημον, which could be translated wilderness or desert, but also a lonely or desolate area generally.

We do not know exactly where the magi saw the top forearm of Scorpio, but Venus would have gone past it at a point very close to the 1,260th day. The margin of error is just a few days. Thus, we have seen several arguments pointing in one clear direction. The woman clearly left her hiding place on the 1,260th day, or very close to that date. We have no reason to doubt that this story is related to that of Venus seeking strength in her hiding place until the gods awarded victory to Amurru – or to put it differently, when there was peace on earth, when the gods turned their goodwill towards men.

To many people, especially those who have Christian values but do not consider themselves Christians, Christmas is a message of peace on earth. According to Luke, this message was delivered by the same angel that heralded the baby's birth, and we have seen that Venus is the star that told of the difficult birth and then heralded the birth nine months later. In doing this, Venus also spoke of the war against the previous king. It would be natural for the magi to ask how long the war would be, and according to Enuma Anu Enlil, Venus had the answer as to when there would be peace on earth: after a struggle against evil of 1,260 days, or three and a half years.

A critical reader might wonder how the magi could have known about the position of Venus in advance. This is a good question, and fortunately also simple to answer. Venus has a very regular

---

[131] White (2014), p. 229.
[132] Koch (2015), p. 141. (Quoted in chapter 2.4)

pattern, and approximately every eight years the pattern repeats itself. The magi would have had diaries telling them how the planets had moved in recent years. If they had consulted these diaries, they could have seen when Venus last had her secondary stop in the secret place. By knowing the last time she herald peace, it would then just be a matter of calculating forwards to find the next time: by finding the secondary stop on this occasion and adding five days for the turn, the result would fit perfectly. Perhaps the magi had even noted in their diaries the moment when Venus left Scorpio and entered Ophiuchus, above Scorpio.

An alternative interpretation is that the magi did not count from the 17th of June but from perhaps the 15th of June, when the sign told them that Amurru would fight against them. The 1260th day could then have been chosen as the day when Venus started to move out of her hiding place, which could be seen as she has stopped hiding. Actually, in all the five texts mentioning that a planet is in its secret place, the planet is in Scorpio or Libra and standing still.[133] If a planet being in its secret place is a combination of location and state, the calculation 1,260 days could be an exact calculation from the signal of war to Venus stopping and starting to move again.

7.6.8 The woman and the baby snatcher

So far, the omens and events in the sky were in full accordance with Revelation 12. The Bible also mentions the dragon/serpent wanting to devour the child.

> 2 She was with child and cried out in labor and in pain to give birth. 3 Then another sign appeared in heaven: There was a great red dragon with seven heads and ten horns, and seven diadems on his heads. 4 His tail drew a third of the stars of heaven, and threw them to the

---

[133] Rochberg (1998), p. 69ff, 77f, 89ff, 97ff, 109f. Jupiter is mentioned three times: in Scorpi, Libra and Virgin. The text where Jupiter is in Virgin (p. 97ff) must be treated as a mistake; since the magi wrongly says that Jupiter is in Libra.

earth. The dragon stood before the woman who was ready to give birth, to devour her Child as soon as He was born.[134]

The basic story is that a child is going to be born and a dragon wants to attack it. Some will probably suggest that the magi expected the demoness Lamashtu, who was originally a goddess. She liked eating human flesh, especially unborn and newly born babies and their mothers. Her interest in human flesh resulted in her being thrown down to earth, just as the dragon was in the midst of the heavenly battle. It may not have been the smartest thing to throw a child-eating demon down to earth, but this is what the myths tell us took place.

It is possible that if the magi knew the story of Lamashtu it might have influenced how they looked on the dragon, and they could have included her in their thinking. But if so, it would be very hard to prove. As mentioned above, the use of clay tablets was diminishing at this point, so we cannot tell if Lamashtu was known and feared during the magi's time as she had been centuries earlier. Either way, for this study it is sufficient to recognise that the dragon attacks the woman and is brought down to earth.

However, one cannot exclude the idea that the demoness was part of the story told by the magi. John the Presbyter has obviously given the whole event his own Christian interpretation. To him, it would be natural to interpret the signs in a different way to the magi. If the signs were originally from God, then if they contained parts that did not fit the Christian belief system, it would be natural for John the Presbyter to see the parts that did not fit as being mistakes made by the magi. Revelation does not exclude the idea that Lamashtu was a part of this story; and if she was, she would have fought on the dragon's side, against the angels and the archangel Michael.

---

[134] The Bible (MEV), Revelation 12:2–4.

7.6.9 Snatched to heaven

In Revelation we find the following passage about the birth:

> She gave birth to a male Child, "who was to rule all nations with an iron scepter." And her Child was caught up to God and to His throne.[135]

The words "caught up to God" are not the same as the words used when Christ returns to heaven; thus, they are probably not intended to be about the ascension of Christ.

It is more likely that the child is caught up to God in the meaning that the child is caught into God's care. The throne of God cannot be seen in heaven. No such constellation is known. The clue to solving this text is that the child of the Virgin – that is, the goddess Ninhursag – is Ninurta, who is represented by Saturn. In other words, Ninurta or Saturn represents the child in the heavens. Saturn is also the representation of the heir to the throne in divination.

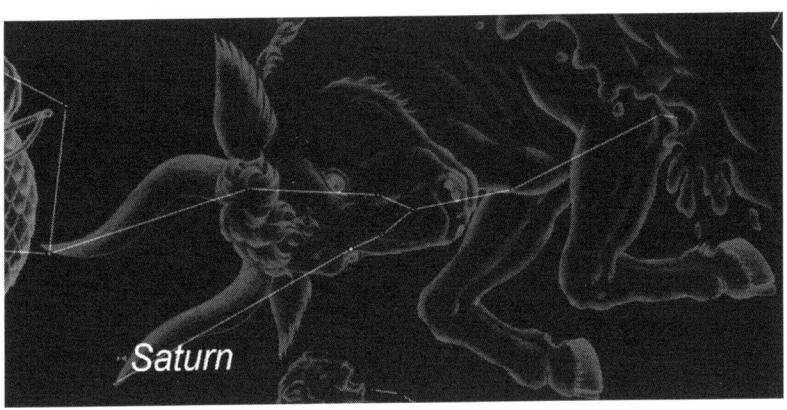

Figure 18. Saturn in the Bull on 17th June 2 BC [136]

On 17th June 2 BC, Saturn was between the horns of the Bull. Marduk, the Bull, was the principal god in theory, and also Ninurta's father (see Chapter 5.5). Thus, the child was under the protection

---

[135] Bible (MEV), Revelation 12:5.
[136] Image created with Starry Night software; see https://starrynight.com.

of the highest god, in the place where Marduk had his place in heaven (see Figure 18). So to say that the child was snatched up to God and his throne, would be an appropriate way to describe the location of Saturn in the Bull.

7.6.10 The woman and the flood

We have already seen that the sign of 17th June 2 BC included an omen about a severe flood (see Chapter 7.6.6). John the Presbyter saw this as being directed against the woman. The magi would have seen it as being directed towards Mesopotamia.

John the Presbyter located some events in the sky and some on earth. He probably understood that the first event (the woman going to her secret place) was a celestial event, but he located the second event (the warning about the flood) on earth, where the dragon uses the flood as a weapon against the woman.

7.7 Conclusion

Several theories have already been put forward as to what the Star of Bethlehem might have been. We have seen that these theories are often based on what we as modern people see as rare phenomena. In this book, an alternative theory has been put forward, which builds on Larson's incomplete theory about Revelation 12 and the astronomical events of 13th September 3 BC and 17th June 2 BC.

In this chapter, we have seen that the full events in the skies on the two dates, and other events related to them, can be explained by referencing Enuma Anu Enlil, astronomical events, and Babylonian religion and culture. We can understand why the magi went to Jerusalem: they wanted their omens to come true – that a newborn king would conquer Babylonia and establish a new kingdom sanctioned by the highest gods. When they arrived in Jerusalem, they were directed to Bethlehem, and as they went down the terrain towards it, Jupiter was seen southward in front of them, always in the general direction of their path. When they arrived, they saw the sign about peace among nations.

The lion, the angel/man, the eagle and the bull, all together told the story of the new king, and thus, the four of them were witnesses to the newly born king. These signs were observed and interpreted by people who did not have the Jewish faith, and they were led to Christ.

A critical reader might think that since the planets are the representatives for the main gods in Babylonia, any theory would be bound to contain the four creatures of the gospels. Although this may be the case, a theory would not be sufficient to merely contain the planets; it must also be able to explain the prediction of a newborn prince in Judah who was going to become the king of the world (this was the royal title in Persia and Mesopotamia at the time).

The events of 13th September 3 BC and 17th June 2 BC are in themselves the best explanation as to why the magi would have decided to travel to Jerusalem. That the events in the sky and the interpretation of them can be found in Revelation is strong evidence that these events were the background to the story of the Star of Bethlehem.

The combination of these events on these two dates is extremely rare. Thus, if Revelation 12 rests on these observations, it rests on observations 2 och 3 BC. There is no irrefutable proof that the magi went to Jerusalem and visited Christ in Bethlehem for the reasons outlined above; but there is sufficient evidence to say that these astronomical events were very likely to have been behind the story of the Star of Bethlehem.

It could still, of course, be argued that John the Presbyter knew about divination and might have made the whole story up. We shall examine this idea further in Chapter 10, but first we will take a closer look at Zoroastrianism.

8 Zoroastrianism

Zoroastrianism is a religion that is often used to explain the background of Judaism as well as Christianity. It is claimed that the scriptures in Zoroastrianism are much older than the Christian and Jewish holy books. The similarities between some beliefs in Zoroastrianism and beliefs in the Bible are said to be because the Bible has borrowed concepts from Zoroastrianism.

Since many people do not want to believe in the teachings of Christianity, they can be quick to adopt such thoughts, although they rarely look at these thoughts with sound scepticism.

8.1 The Zoroastrian sources

The truth is that the origins of Zoroastrianism are unknown, and the majority of its surviving texts are from a time when Zoroastrians lived side by side with Christians and Jews. The oldest preserved copies of the Avesta – as the largest part of Zoroastrian religious texts are collectively called – are actually from the Middle Ages, and thus about eight hundred years younger than the oldest Christian texts.[137] A full examination must therefore look at the possibility that the Zoroastrians borrowed from their Jewish and Christian neighbours.

The oldest Zoroastrian texts are considerably older, however. They are called the Gathas, and they are a kind of liturgical song, generally thought to have come from the founder of the religion, Zoroaster. Other texts, not so old, are the Videvdat.

Zaehner writes about the status of these sources:

> The language of the Avesta very soon seems to have become a purely liturgical language which was no

---

[137] Zaehner (1961), p. 25.

longer spoken and very imperfectly understood. Thus whereas in the Gathas we feel that we cannot explain it due to our own ignorance, we can feel tolerably certain that the in the Cidevdat what appear to be gross grammatical blunders are genuinely so. Indeed, in the Videvdat we have the impression that the authors are not only writing in a language that is not their own, but are doing so in one of the rudiments of whose grammar they had quite failed to master.[138]

Excited rather than dismayed by the uncertainties that met them wherever they turn, scholars have built the most elaborate and improbable religious structures which they would have us believe are authentic representations of Zoroastrianism.[139]

Thus, we should be very cautious about claims explaining how Zoroastrianism influenced Judaism and Christianity. It seems more likely that a religion whose followers were not able to read its own religious texts would have imported concepts from its Jewish and Christian neighbours, rather than the other way around.

8.2 Zoroaster

Zoroaster is thought to have lived in Persia in around 630–550 BC. He seems to have been opposed to the native religion, Mithraism. Like his Jewish parallel figure, Moses, he seems to have believed in one supreme god, with the other gods either being transformed into the supreme being's helpers, or being removed from the picture completely and branded as heathens. In this respect, Zoroastrianism is similar to the Jewish religion. However, when new religions replace old ones, it is common for the older gods to live on in the public imagination as some kind of lesser gods or spirits. So the fact that this happened in the Jewish religion as well as in Zoroastrianism

---

[138] Zaehner (1961), p. 26.
[139] Zaehner (1961), p. 29.

does not prove that either of them influenced the other. This is a human pattern that is repeated around the globe.

Contrary to common belief, Zoroaster is not said to have been born of a virgin. Further, the idea that a saviour should be born every 800 years after a great conjunction seems to have emerged perhaps 600 years or so after the birth of Christ.

8.3 The impact of Zoroaster

The impact of Zoroaster was not great. His religion appears to have been popular for a time, but his early followers seem to have mixed his original ideas with Mithraism. The Persian king Darius worshipped many gods, according to his own inscriptions, and yet he would have been a monotheist if he had been a Zoroastrian. Zaehner calls Darius' religion "primitive Zoroastrianism".[140]

The later Persian kings might have been monotheists, but this assumption rests on the fact that their inscriptions do not mention other gods. This is an argument from silence, however, which can never be as strong as direct evidence showing what they actually did or believed.

In the second and third centuries AD, we see the rise of a sect within Zoroastrianism called Zurvanism. They believed in their own form of astrology where all the planets had a negative influence. This astrology was thus not Greek astrology, but rather their own invention. This sect influenced Zoroastrianism, but their beliefs do not seem to be in accordance with Zoroaster's original beliefs.[141]

Thus, an examination of these sources suggests that the Zoroastrian priests did not practise astrology, and even if they had, it would not have rested on Greek or Babylonian ideas.

---

[140] Zaehner (1961), p. 157.
[141] Zaehner (1961), pp. 205–206, 214.

9 The Star of Bethlehem in a historical context

When discussing the historicity of the Star of Bethlehem it is not sufficient to study the stars. We must also examine if the biblical story is compatible with history. The main obstacle to this is the taxation by Augustus:

> 1 In those days a decree went out from Caesar Augustus that the entire inhabited earth should be taxed. 2 This taxation was first made when Quirinius was governor of Syria. 3 And everyone went to his own city to be taxed. 4 So Joseph also departed from the city of Nazareth in Galilee to the City of David which is called Bethlehem, in Judea, because he was of the house and lineage of David, 5 to be taxed with Mary, his betrothed wife, who was with child. 6 So while they were there, the day came for her to give birth. 7 And she gave birth to her firstborn Son, and wrapped Him in strips of cloth, and laid Him in a manger, because there was no room for them in the inn.[142]

The taxation was the reason for Mary and Joseph to travel to Bethlehem. Thus, the birth of Christ must have happened after the taxation, according to the Bible. The first know taxation by the Romans was carried out in AD 6, but this is too late to fit in with the story of the Star of Bethlehem. According to Luke 3:23, Christ was about thirty years old when he was baptised, and he was crucified a few years after this, sometime between AD 30 and AD 35. This time span is generally accepted, and we do not need to examine it further. However, if Christ was in his early or mid-thirties

---

[142] The Bible (MEV), Luke 2:1–7.

when he was crucified, he must have been born well before the taxation in AD 6. Due to this, it is generally agreed that Christ was born in 1 BC or earlier.

The Bible also connects the birth of Christ with king Herod:

> Now after Jesus was born in Bethlehem of Judea in the days of Herod the king, wise men came from the east to Jerusalem, 2 saying, "Where is He who was born King of the Jews? For we have seen His star in the east and have come to worship Him." 3 When Herod the king heard these things, he was troubled, and all Jerusalem with him. 4 And when he had gathered all the chief priests and scribes of the people together, he inquired of them where Christ should be born. 5 They told him, "In Bethlehem of Judea, for this is what the prophet wrote: 6 'And you, Bethlehem, in the land of Judah, are no longer least among the princes of Judah; for out of you shall come a Governor, who will shepherd My people Israel.'" 7 Then Herod, when he had privately called the wise men, carefully inquired of them what time the star appeared. 8 And he sent them to Bethlehem and said, "Go and search diligently for the young Child, and when you have found Him, bring me word again, so that I may come and worship Him also." 9 When they heard the king, they departed. And the star which they saw in the east went before them until it came and stood over where the young Child was. 10 When they saw the star, they rejoiced with great excitement. 11 And when they came into the house, they saw the young Child with Mary, His mother, and fell down and worshipped Him. And when they had opened their treasures, they presented gifts to Him: gold, frankincense, and myrrh. 12 But being warned in

a dream that they should not return to Herod, they returned to their own country by another route.

Matthew is clear that the magi visited King Herod and that his son Archelaus succeeded him in Judah, but with the title of ethnarch (see Chapter 4.8). The actual year of Christ's birth is dependent on when Herod died, since the Bible states that the magi met him in Jerusalem. The present scholarly opinion is that Herod died in 4 BC; other opinions range from 5 BC to 1 BC, but the largest consensus is for 4 BC.

The date for Herod's death is mainly based on the writings of the Jewish writer Josephus. Hutchinson goes to great lengths to prove that the regnal years in Josephus' writings are not reliable. He then focuses on Josephus' claim that Herod died some weeks after an eclipse of the moon; he believes that this eclipse is most likely to have been the one on the 9th/10th January 1 BC, and that Herod died on 27th/28th January 1 BC. Another eclipse of the moon occurred in 4 BC, but Hutchinson dismisses it, since it was only a partial eclipse, and therefore not likely to draw attention.[143]

9.1 Chapter outline

The theory in this book is that the magi saw events in the sky in 3 BC and 2 BC and then travelled to Jerusalem, arriving in Bethlehem on around 25th December 2 BC. If this is true, the death of Herod must have occurred in 1 BC or the Bible is wrong about who the magi met in Jerusalem.

The study of Herod and Quirinius is thus essential when studying whether the story of the Star of Bethlehem is compatible with history. However, when studying history it is important to evaluate the sources. What sources do we have, when were they written, and how reliable are they?

---

[143] Hutchinson (2015), p. 308.

In this chapter we shall begin by looking more deeply at how history was recorded in Roman times. Next, we shall examine our sources – the main one being the Jewish author Josephus, who was born long after the death of Herod. How good is he as a source, and what are *his* sources?

Next, we shall look more closely at what we know about King Herod, as Josephus presents it. How well does his story fit with what we know from other sources? Josephus correlates events in Herod's life with major events that happened at the same time, thus we have a way to examine how reliable Josephus is. In this study, the story of Herod's life is not the main interest; the main purpose is to evaluate Josephus as a historical source. Only after understanding our sources can we decide how reliable our knowledge of the timing of Herod's death is – and thus how likely it is that the story of the Star of Bethlehem as presented in this book is historically accurate.

This book will argue that our sources are good concerning descriptions of Herod's life, but very poor concerning his death. The reliability of our sources drops considerably some years before the death of Herod. Josephus' earlier writings of Herod's life seem to have rested on a written account by an eyewitness who had been in the service of Herod; in contrast, Josephus' later writings concerning the death of Herod seem to have relied solely on oral traditions, so their reliability is considerably lower.

9.2 Historical sources for dating the death of Herod/birth of Christ

How accurately do we know when Herod died? What are the facts? It is widely known that Ancient Rome was an early civilisation with a central bureaucracy. It is therefore easy to believe that the basic facts about rulers were well documented. However, we must not forget that Ancient Rome ceased to exist, and that prior to that it burned, and changed political leadership several times. Every such event would have caused a loss of archived data. Further, although Herod was a king, he was not a very important ally to Rome. Under such circumstances, it is not surprising that data has been lost.

What we know from Rome is mostly what ancient authors have recorded. Some of these authors write about times prior to their own lives, sometimes centuries before they were born. Some historians base their books on previous authors; this means that although two ancient authors might seem to support each other, the reality might be that the later author has only read, and at best copied or at worst interpreted, the previous work. Sometimes an author writes about the work of another author that he has read, whom we know of, but whose work has been completely lost.

The suggested theories of the time of Herod's death have been based on three main sources of evidence: the historical works and chronological facts provided by Josephus; an eclipse of the moon; and some coins.

We do not have any written preserved sources other than Josephus concerning Herod's death – excluding later historians, who build their accounts on Josephus' account. Josephus is also our only source concerning the taxation that occurred when Quirinius was governor. Josephus is also the one who mentions the eclipse of the moon occurring close to the time of Herod's death.

Sometimes archaeology can help us by providing data in the form of objects, such as dated inscriptions and coins found in the remains of conquered and destroyed cities, which can give us better dates and confirmation about things that authors from much later periods have written about. But when it comes to King Herod, we do not possess any archaeological data that can help us tell when he died, even if we will see that some coins are of interest.

Since the timing of the death of King Herod is of such great importance when trying to explain the Star of Bethlehem, the attempts to date his death have been numerous, and have resulted in theories that are in obvious conflict with each other. The suggested years for the death have been 5 BC, 4 BC, 3 BC, 2 BC and 1 BC, all of which have resulted from theories based on Josephus.

9.3 Ancient counting/dating methods

In order to understand and evaluate our sources, we must first examine how time spans were calculated in ancient sources. Their form of counting was different from the one we use today, which may seem surprising, but fact is that not all people count years the same and the manner of calculation vary in different cultures.

The system we are most familiar with is where we count complete years from one date to another. So if someone is born in early 2016 and moves to another city in late 2018 we would say that the child is two years old when he moves (he has not yet reached his third birthday). However, we could also say that the child has lived in the city in which he was born for three years. In this case, we refer to the three calendar years: 2016, 2017 and 2018. Therefore, depending on whether we are counting complete years or calendar years, our calculation will be different, and no one could say that either way of counting is wrong.

A similar problem is the difference between *exclusive counting* and *inclusive counting*. We would say that the summer Olympics are held every fourth year, but the ancients would have said that it was held every fifth year. Using "exclusive counting", we exclude the first year (the year of the current summer Olympics) and treat it as year zero, then we count on four years and end up with the year of the next summer Olympics. In contrast, the ancients used "inclusive counting" and would instead have treated the first year as year one, so that the next Olympics would start in the fifth year.

9.3.1 Regnal years

To correctly interpret ancient sources, we need to be aware that there also were two different systems for counting regnal years (the years of a monarch's reign) in the Greco-Roman world.

Figure 19. Emperor Galba minted coins in his regnal year 2(B),[144] even though he was emperor for only seven months. [145]

When Herod lived and at the time when Josephus wrote, the system used in Rome was to see regnal years as the number of different calendar years in which a monarch had reigned; that is, the first regnal year is normally the actual year, according to the local calendar, that someone ascended the throne. So even if a new monarch came to power on New Year's Eve and died the following day, that monarch would still have had two regnal years. Emperor Galba, who succeeded Nero on 9th June AD 68 and died on 15th January AD 69, is a good example of this way of counting. He reigned for little more than seven months, but is still described as having two regnal years; he even minted a coin dated "ETOUC B", that is, "Year 2" (see Figure 19).

---

[144] The year is written in Greek, which used letters as numerals. A was 1, B was 2, etc.
[145] Photograph © www.forumancientcoins.com; used with permission obtained on 26th December 2016.

This method for counting the length of a reign is called the *Egyptian system*, which contrasts with the method of counting the span of a reign from the exact date of the ascension to the throne – the *Macedonian system*. In the period relevant to our study, the Egyptian system was used in Rome.[146]

However, to complicate things even further, the Egyptian system will be dependent on which calendar was used. If Josephus or his sources used the Egyptian system it is crucial to understand when the year started, as this naturally marks the point at which one regnal year changes to the next. For example, the Roman calendar, which starts its new year on 1st January, was not widely used at the time; in Egypt, the civil year started in the autumn. Accordingly, the break between regnal years was in January in Rome and in the autumn in Egypt.

Did Josephus use the Jewish, Roman or perhaps the Greek calendar? When it comes to months, Josephus uses Jewish months but also Attic (Athenian) and Macedonian month names. Thus, it is not obvious what calendar he is using. Another confusing thing is how he numbers months. In Judah months were numbered with Nisan, that is the month of Passover in spring, as month number one, and this seems to be how months are numbered in Josephus' books. Thus, anytime a month is referred to by only a number, we should assume that the Jewish numbering is intended, since this is the only numbering we can confidently identify. This numbering is in fact still used today, even though the (civil) Jewish year begins in the autumn. The Jewish year therefore does not start with month number one, which might seem puzzling to non-Jews.

9.3.2 Consular years

Another way of dating in ancient historical texts was to use consular years. Before the time of Emperor Augustus, and during the first half of his life, dating in Rome was marked according to who the

---

[146] Bagnall (2009) pp. 182–183.

consuls were. Roman consuls normally sat for one year, beginning at the start of the Roman year in January. Two consuls were elected for each year, and if someone died or had to leave office, the Senate elected a new consul for the rest of the year. If a consul sat for more than one period, the dating was simply marked as referencing the consul's second or third year and so on.

9.3.3 Years since Rome was founded

Another system was to date events according to the year since the founding of Rome. However, the normal dating process in Rome was to reference who was consul.

9.3.4 Olympiads

The Greeks also developed their own dating system of Olympiads, based on the length of time between the Olympic Games. The Greek city states had different calendars, which meant that the new year did not begin at the same time everywhere. In Athens, the Attic year was used, and the Attic year is thought to have started with the first new moon after the summer solstice.[147] In Macedonia, which had a Greek culture, the New Year was generally celebrated in October. Other calendars were also used in other Greek areas.

However, the Greek states had the common tradition of holding the Olympic Games every fourth year (or every fifth year, as they would put it; see Chapter 9.3).

> Ancient historians date by Olympiad by giving both the number of the Olympiad and the year within the cycle, 1–4 (the Olympiad itself was held on year 1 [within the cycle]).[148]

The first Olympiad lasted from the summer of 776 BC to the summer of 772 BC, at least according to ancient historians. To us

---

[147] Burgess (1999), p. 33.
[148] See http://www.polysyllabic.com/?q=calhistory/earlier/greek.

this might seem to be five years, but we must remember that the year began in the summer. The 184th Olympiad was 732 years later (183 periods of four years): from the summer of 44 BC to the summer of 40 BC.

This might seem to be a good system, since it is did not rest on a certain calendar but on the common Olympic Games. However, things were not that simple. For people using the Macedonian calendar, an Olympiad would not have started in the year of the Olympic Games, but rather in the fourth year of the Olympiad. This problem was solved by counting Olympiads from the October of the year before the games. In this way the Olympic games would start in the first year of the Olympiad. The Greek historian Eusebius used this method, and thus his dates are often one year too early compared with the Attic Olympiads.

9.3.5 How important were dates?

If we read Livy, one of the most important Roman historians, we notice that the dating of years and events was not an important concern in ancient times. History was more like a saga, a story of what had happened in the past; consuls or Olympiads were occasionally mentioned in order to keep the reader informed of roughly when something happened.

Thus, the dating system was not a priority at that point in time. To us, a book about history would be highly unsatisfactory if it did not contain clear dates, but this is only how we see things with our modern eyes.

9.4 Josephus and his sources

Let us now take a closer look at Josephus. Josephus was born in AD 37 and lived to around AD 100. He wrote two books of interest to this study: *The Wars of the Jews* (*c.*AD 75) and *Antiquities of the Jews* (*c.*AD 94). In the first, he focuses on the wars of Herod and his descendants down to the fall of Jerusalem in AD 70 (see Chapter 4.8).

He clearly had to rely on some kind of source when writing the history of King Herod, and in his writings, Josephus mentions the historians Nicolaus of Damascus, Livy and Strabo. All of them were active during the time of King Herod, and they died in the second and third decades of the first century AD. Thus, they lived in a similar period of time, both to each other and to Herod himself. Nicolaus of Damascus worked for King Herod, and then for Herod's son Archelaus during the early part of his rule as ethnarch. Thus, Nicolaus was close to Herod and able to provide first-hand information.

Since Josephus refers to Nicolaus, we have every reason to believe that Josephus' writings are based on an eyewitness account, up to the point when Nicolaus' history ended. After that, Josephus would have had poorer sources concerning events that happened outside his own lifetime. This is evidenced by the quality of his writing at these different times. Josephus is detailed in his narrative up to the time when Nicolaus moved to Rome,[149] then his information becomes scarce up to the time when he was active himself in the Jewish revolt against the Romans.

We cannot tell exactly when Nicolaus of Damascus wrote his history. According to Josephus, it would have been during Herod's lifetime, and in such a case Josephus' account of Herod's death would not rest on Nicolaus, but on some source unknown to us. Josephus claims his own family traditions as one of his sources, but such oral traditions are poor sources for history, since dates and the order of events are often obscured over the years.

---

[149] See http://www.jewishencyclopedia.com/articles/11524-nicholas-of-damascus-nicolaus-damascenus.

This is what Josephus says about both Nicolaus and his own family as sources of information:

> For he [Nicolaus] wrote in Herod's lifetime, and under his reign, and so as to please him, and as a servant to him, touching upon nothing but what tended to his glory, and openly excusing many of his notorious crimes, and very diligently concealing them. ... Indeed, a man, as I said, may have a great deal to say by way of excuse for Nicolaus; for he did not so properly write this as a history for others, as somewhat that might be subservient to the king himself. As for ourselves, who come of a family nearly allied to the Asamonean kings, and on that account have an honorable place, which is the priesthood, we think it indecent to say any thing that is false about them, and accordingly we have described their actions after an unblemished and upright manner. And although we reverence many of Herod's posterity, who still reign, yet do we pay a greater regard to truth than to them.[150]

Josephus was one of the leading fighters in the Jewish revolt leading up to the fall of Jerusalem; thus, he is probably reliable in these details as well, even if he might leave out details that would be unpopular for his Roman readers, and perhaps dangerous to write. However, these events are beyond the scope of this book.

Josephus' dates about Herod must be taken seriously as long as he relies on Nicolaus, but not without critical analysis. We must also ask ourselves what Josephus did with Nicolaus' dates: did he alter them, and if so, what was he trying to achieve with his alterations?

---

[150] Josephus (*Antiquities of the Jews*), Book XVI, Chapter 7:1.

9.4.1 How does Josephus count regnal years?

Emperor Galba had two regnal years; an ancient historian could therefore date an event by saying that something happened in Galba's second year. Josephus uses the same model, and describes events as happening in a certain year of Herod's reign. However, the counting of regnal years can be confusing to a modern reader, as we saw above. Saying that Galba had two regnal years is not the same as suggesting that Galba reigned for two years. This confusion between regnal years and the length of a monarch's reign is very common when discussing Josephus' dates. In fact, it is very easy to demonstrate how Josephus counted how long a king or emperor had reigned. We just have to look at the known dates.

Emperor Tiberius, for instance, reigned from 18th September AD 14 until 16th March AD 37, which would be 22 years, 5 months and 28 days, which is almost what Josephus says. He actually calculates this to 22 years, 6 months and 3 days, which means he accidentally counted from 16th September to 18th March.[151] The regnal years were AD 14 to AD 37, which would make 24 regnal years. Another example is Emperor Claudius, who reigned from 24th January AD 41 until 13th October AD 54, which is 13 years, 8 months and 20 days, exactly as Josephus says. The regnal years were AD 41 to AD 54, which would make 14 regnal years.[152]

So while Josephus uses regnal years in his dating of events, we can see that when he calculates the length of a monarch's reign, he does so from the date the reign started to the date the reign ended. From a mathematical point of view, regnal years and years someone has been in office must be treated separately. As seen above the regnal years are often one or even two years more than the calculated years someone has been in office. Tiberius was emperor 22 years but had 24 regnal years.

---

[151] Josephus (*The Wars of the Jews*), Book II, Chapter 9:1.
[152] Josephus (*Antiquities of the Jews*), Book XX, Chapter 8:1.

A critical reader might argue: how do we know that Josephus always calculated regnal years in the same fashion? While it is true that we cannot know this for certain, we do know that the Egyptian system was the method used in Rome at the time, so this is the most likely interpretation. Further, it is more sensible to assume consistency on Josephus' part than to try to prove that he sometimes used one method and sometimes another.

9.4.2 Calendar systems used by Josephus

Josephus does not have one single calendar system. He uses Olympiads as well as consular years and the regnal years of emperors and kings. Further, he uses Jewish month names, Macedonian month names and even Attic month names, as said above (see Chapter 9.3.1).

Ancient Greek historians stated both Olympiads and years within the Olympiads. However, the Olympiad dates are crippled in Josephus' books, since he does not give the year within the Olympiad that something happened (apart from once). A critical analysis must therefore include a study of what his source was, and whether it is likely that the source lacked the full description of the Olympiad and the year within the Olympiad. If, however, it is more likely that the source had a full date, we must examine why Josephus chose to remove these dates, and thereby make his dating less precise.

The last Olympiad mentioned by Josephus is the 192nd Olympiad (12–8 BC). However, Eusebius, who lived from approximately AD 260 to AD 340, also used the Olympiad method of dating, so we know that this method was still used when Josephus lived.

Olympiads are mentioned eleven times in *Antiquities of the Jews*, beginning with the 153rd Olympiad (168–164 BC), when the Seleucid king Antiochus IV conquered Jerusalem and plundered the holy temple in Jerusalem. In connection with this, the 153rd Olympiad is mentioned twice and the restoration of the temple is said to have occurred in the 154th Olympiad. Macedonian month names are used in connection with these dates, and in one case both the Jewish and Macedonian month names are used.[153]

The next Olympiad mentioned by Josephus is the 162nd (132–128 BC), when Hyrcanus became the high priest. He was attacked by the Seleucid king Antiochus VII and had to surrender, but later, when Antiochus VII died, Hyrcanus managed to make Judah independent.[154]

After this, Josephus references the 177th Olympiad, and this time he mentions the year within the Olympiad: the third year (70–69 BC), when Hyrcanus II became high priest. In this case, the consuls of Rome are also mentioned, and said to be "Quintus Hortensius and Quintus Metellus".[155] In connection with this episode, Josephus comments on Nicolaus of Damascus and his description of events. As this is the only occasion on which the year of the Olympiad is mentioned, and since Nicolaus is explicitly mentioned, it is likely that the date came from Nicolaus of Damascus.

Since it is also likely that Josephus' other Olympiad dates came from Nicolaus of Damascus, and since the year within the Olympiad is mentioned this early, we must suspect that Nicolaus also used them in later dates. Since Nicolaus of Damascus was an eyewitness and worked for King Herod, these dates must have been very reliable and accurate.

Olympiads are also mentioned during Herod's reign, but not in connection with his death. After Herod, no Olympiads are mentioned, even if it would have been a simple thing for Josephus to include them. It could be argued that Josephus did not need Olympiads after Herod, since he could date events with the regnal

---

[153] Josephus (*Antiquities of the Jews*), Book XII, Chapters 5:4 and 7:6.
[154] Josephus (*Antiquities of the Jews*), Book XIII, Chapter 8:2.
[155] Josephus (*Antiquities of the Jews*), Book XIV, Chapter 1:2.

year of the emperor instead. However, he could also have dated events with the regnal years of Augustus during Herod's reign, but he did not.

Josephus did not try to find Olympiads for the events in his earlier books; nor did he try to calculate the Olympiads after King Herod. It seems clear that the Olympiad dating was something that the sources provided, rather than something that Josephus had put effort into calculating himself; but since he seems to have crippled the dates, we must ask ourselves whether perhaps he did not agree with the dates in his sources.

It is likely that Josephus compiled his text from his sources and occasionally translated the months to Jewish names; the quote below is a good example, where he translates the Macedonian month name "Apelleus" to the Jewish name "Chasleu":

> Now it came to pass, after two years, in the hundred forty and fifth year, on the twenty-fifth day of that month which is by us called Chasleu, and by the Macedonians Apelleus, in the hundred and fifty-third olympiad, that the king came up to Jerusalem.[156]

As said above, the histories of Strabo and Nicolaus are lost, apart from some smaller quotes. Thus, their dating system cannot be checked. However, Josephus also mentions Polybius, a Greek historian, who died in approximately 118 BC. Polybius' account ends in approximately 150 BC, as he says in his own epilogue:

> I undertook to make a fresh beginning from this date, i.e. the 139th Olympiad, and henceforth to deal with the general history of the whole world, classing it under Olympiads, dividing those into years and taking a comparative view of the succession of events until the capture of Carthage, the battle of the Achaeans and

---

[156] Josephus (*Antiquities of the Jews*), Book XII, Chapter 5:4.

Romans at the Isthmus and the consequent settlement of Greece.[157]

Polybius never uses month names – only Olympiads. From the 139th Olympiad, as he says above, he tries to include the year of the Olympiad. Unfortunately, the majority of his books are lost, so it is difficult to say how well he succeeded in his efforts. In his accounts of Roman history, he added the names of the consuls. However, several of the Olympiads mentioned by Josephus occurred after the death of Polybius; thus, Josephus must have received these Olympiads from another author, such as Nicolaus of Damascus or Strabo. Both authors' historical books have been largely lost, but we know that Strabo uses Olympiads in his book *Geographica*.

Nicolaus of Damascus is first mentioned as a source already in the first book of *Antiquities of the Jews*, while Strabo is first mentioned in Book 13, in connection with events in around 130 BC. However, Strabo's historical account begins where Polybius' ends. Thus, Strabo might have thought of his own account as a continuation of Polybius' work, and for that reason he may have used the same style of dating: mentioning Roman consuls and Olympiads, and the year within the Olympiad, if he knew it.

It could be that Nicolaus used Strabo as a source until approximately 30 BC, when Strabo's account is thought to have ended. Nicolaus probably then compiled several sources into one, though he might have relied heavily on Strabo, at least concerning some episodes prior to his own time:

> Now Nicolaus of Damascus, and Strabo of Cappadocia, both describe the expeditions of Pompey and Gabinius against the Jews, while neither of them say anything new which is not in the other.[158]

---

[157] Polybius, Book 39.
[158] Josephus (*Antiquities of the Jews*), Book XIV, Chapter 6:4.

No consul is mentioned during Herod's reign after the approximate time when Strabo's work ended, which suggests that Nicolaus got consular dates from Strabo, and then did not use them, since consular dates were not used in Judah. Thus, it is possible to conclude that Josephus is relying on Nicolaus, who in turn probably relies on Strabo and older historians. This means that Josephus has no written source describing the death of Herod. The holy temple in Jerusalem had been destroyed when Josephus started to write his history books, and he also lived in Rome, so it is not likely that he had direct access to material from the temple.

Researchers have tried to discover the sources that Nicolaus of Damascus used by examining the remaining fragments of his own writings. It was suggested above that he used Strabo, mainly because Josephus found that they said the same things, and Nicolaus wrote later than Strabo. However, Nicolaus' only identified source was Ctesias of Cnidus, who lived in the fifth century BC.[159]

The author Biltcliffe has examined Nicolaus and Strabo, and states:

> The close verbal, if not stylistic, similarity between Strabo's and Nicolaus' version of the incest of Piasus with his daughter Larisa underlines the probability that these frequent "variants" are simply due to Nicolaus' source. To determine his sources for Greek history with certainty is impossible. … Since he seems to have used only Ctesias for Oriental history, it is probable that he restricted himself to certain "standard" authors of Greek affairs also. … Otherwise, it is probable that Strabo was dependent on Nicolaus, since it can be proved that he used him at least on occasion.[160]

It is strange that Strabo should be dependent on Nicolaus, when the latter wrote later, so this looks like a mistake by Biltcliffe. At any

---

[159] Biltcliffe (1970), p. 39.
[160] Biltcliffe (1970), pp. 130–131, 137.

rate, Biltcliffe has also noticed similarities between Nicolaus of Damascus and Strabo.

We cannot prove the exact relationship between Strabo and Nicolaus of Damascus, but the interesting thing in connection with Josephus is that he himself claims that he had access to both sources and that they were similar. We also have no reason to doubt that both of them used correct Olympiad dating – and yet this is lacking in all cases but one in *Antiquities of the Jews*.

The theory in this book is that Josephus had a clear idea as to when Herod's reign ended: that is, some time before Passover in 4 BC. He then took information from Strabo and Nicolaus of Damascus, but found that the dates provided by them did not fit his own opinion of events. Because of this, he removed the information about the year within the Olympiads.

9.5 The history of King Herod

We shall now examine the history of Herod's reign and how Josephus' version of events relates to what really happened.

In doing so we need to be clear about certain facts from the outset. Herod was king in an area roughly equal to the present state of Israel, including the Palestinian areas. It is generally accepted that Herod's kingdom was later divided between his children. The southern part maintained the name Judah, and was given to Archelaus. Galilea and Perea were given to Antipas. These two areas lay in the middle of Herod's kingdom, but between them was the autonomous area of Decapolis. The north-eastern parts, Iturea and Trachonities, were given to Philip; and a very small area was given to Herod's daughter Salome. It should be noted that the three sons mentioned above are sometimes called Herod Archelaus, Herod Antipas and Herod Philip by some authors.

Herod had many children in addition to those named above. Of primary interest is Antipater, who was executed by Herod shortly before his own death. Antipater appears to have been originally appointed as Herod's successor, but was imprisoned for treason. Two more of Herod's sons were also strangled to death at his orders.

Herod rose to power with the aid of Mark Antony, a Roman general, who was both allied with and a competitor of the future Emperor Augustus. Herod managed to switch his allegiance to Augustus at the very last moment, thus ensuring that he would not fall together with Mark Antony and his mistress, Queen Cleopatra.

We will now look more deeply into some key events in Herod's life, in order to show that Josephus' date for his death is not reliable.

9.5.1 Herod is appointed to be king in 40 BC

The first date that Josephus connects to Herod is the 184th Olympiad (44–40 BC), when Caius Domitius Calvinus and Caius Asinius Pollio were consuls. The names of these consuls limit the year to 40 BC, so this is thought to be the time when Herod was appointed as the king of Judah by the Roman Senate.[161] But can we be more precise about when this happened?

We know that Mark Antony travelled to Italy, where he fought against Augustus in September of that year. The two of them met later that month, and ended hostilities by signing the Treaty of Brundisium; Antony also married Augustus' sister in October. At around this time Herod travelled from Egypt to meet Antony in Italy, though Queen Cleopatra had warned him about some turmoil in Italy and some bad weather. Herod passed through Rhodes on the way, and when he met Antony in Rome, Herod told him some news from Judah. Soon afterwards, Herod was presented to the Senate and appointed as the king of Judah.

Some say that since Cleopatra knew about the turmoil in Italy, someone must have travelled from Italy to Alexandria in September

---

[161] Josephus (*Antiquities of the Jews*), Book XIV, Chapter 14:4–5.

to give her this news. Thus, Herod must have travelled very late in the autumn, it is argued. However, Antony had travelled to Italy due to the civil war there between Augustus and Fulvia, who at that point was Antony's legal wife. Thus, there was turmoil in Italy prior to September, and perhaps Cleopatra was referring to this turmoil.

Cleopatra's warning of bad weather has also been used as an argument to support the case that Herod travelled in the winter. This is not a good argument, however, as the Mediterranean region is known for its bad weather in both autumn and winter.[162]

Since Herod's trip clearly occurred in the autumn or winter, we cannot say for certain when exactly he arrived in Rome. However, since Antony arrived in Rome not earlier than late September, Herod could not have arrived earlier than late September, and due to the warnings of bad weather, he probably arrived in October or later. If the Attic Olympiad system was used, this would have been in the first year of the 185th Olympiad. However, if the Macedonian Olympiads were used, this could have happened in September, the very last month of the 184th Olympiad, according to the Macedonian calendar.

> Antony also feasted Herod the first day of his reign. And thus did this man receive the kingdom, having obtained it on the hundred and eighty-fourth olympiad, when Caius Domitius Calvinus was consul the second time, and Caius Asinius Pollio [the first time].[163]

In other words, we can see that Josephus assigns the appointment of Herod to the first half of the year, if he uses the common Attic Olympiad. If the Macedonian Olympiad is used and if Herod was appointed to be king no later than the very beginning of October, the date will be correct. Macedonian dates where used in the eastern

---

[162] See http://www.cruisecritic.com/articles.cfm?ID=1226.
[163] Josephus (*Antiquities of the Jews*), Book XIV, Chapter 14:5.

parts of the Roman Empire, so it would not be surprising if Nicolaus used them. Strabo also came from the eastern parts.

An observant reader might react to this and say that Macedonian Olympiads began in October the year before the games. However, that is how Eusebius calculates dates. When referring to Macedonian Olympiads, this book does not refer to Eusebius' system, since his system must be treated as an exception rather than the rule.

9.5.2 Herod becomes king in 37 BC

The next Olympiad that Josephus connects to Herod is the 185th (40–36 BC), when Herod actually became king, and when Marcus Agrippa and Caninius Gallus were consuls; that is, in 37 BC:

> This destruction befell the city of Jerusalem when Marcus Agrippa and Caninius Gallus were consuls of Rome, on the hundred eighty and fifth olympiad, on the third month, on the solemnity of the fast, as if a periodical revolution of calamities had returned since that which befell the Jews under Pompey; for the Jews were taken by him on the same day, and this was after twenty-seven years' time.[164]

Jewish months are counted from Passover, so the third month is Sivan, which is in May/June. The ancient Jews had a fast on 23rd Sivan, which might have been the fast mentioned by Josephus in the quote above.[165] Since the Attic year starts with the new moon, just as Jewish months do, the Attic year must start after the month of Sivan. Thus, the correct year that Herod conquered Jerusalem would have been the third year of the 185th Olympiad, in both the Attic and Macedonian way of calculating Olympiads.

---

[164] Josephus (*Antiquities of the Jews*), Book XIV, Chapter 16:4.
[165] See http://www.torahtots.com/timecapsule/thismonth/sivan.htm.

According to Josephus, Herod could have attacked Jerusalem the year before, but he refrained due to the challenges of winter:

> When the rigor of winter was over, Herod removed his army, and came near to Jerusalem, and pitched his camp hard by the city. Now this was the third year since he had been made king at Rome …[166]

How could the year 37 BC be the third year since he had been made king at Rome? If we use a Roman calendar, the third year would be 38 BC. If we apply the Attic calendar we would find that Herod became king in Rome in 40/39 BC (i.e. the Attic year starting year 40 BC and ending in 39 BC), and conquered Jerusalem in 38/37 BC, which would be the third Attic year. However, if the Attic year were used, Herod would have been appointed king by the Senate in the first year of the 185th Olympiad. Thus, the dates are contradictory if the Attic calendar is used. If the Macedonian calendar is used we have to decide on which side of the New Year Herod was appointed king by the Senate. If it happened in the 184th Olympiad it happened before New Year, but then the first year would be 41/40 and the third year 39/38. If, on the other hand, Herod were appointed after the New Year the Olympiad would be wrong.

The only possible solution to this dilemma is if the Macedonian Olympiads are used, as we would suspect Nicolaus to do, and at the same time calculated the years in reign from the Jewish Calendar, as we would expect Herod to do. Herod would then have become king in the Jewish year 40/39 BC but before the Macedonian New Year, and thus still in the 184th Olympiad according to Macedonian calculation.

Someone could say that "the third year since he had been made king…" refers to three years after 40 BC, which will be 37 BC.

---

[166] Josephus (*Antiquities of the Jews*), Book XIV, Chapter 15:14.

However, this is a calculation based on exclusive counting, and is not valid.

Further, Josephus says that Jerusalem fell to Herod on the same day as it fell to Pompey, "after twenty-seven years' time". From 63 BC to 37 BC is twenty-six years, based on exclusive counting. However, the ancients used inclusive counting, as mentioned above (see Chapter 9.3). Thus, the year 63 BC would be the first year of twenty-seven years (think of how the second year of our life starts on our first birthday). Josephus clearly uses inclusive counting in the case of Pompey and assuming that he did so also for Herod is reasonable, since that is the ancient way of counting.

Josephus continuous with describing how the former king of Judah, Antigonus, was sent to Mark Antony in chains after the fall of Jerusalem. He writes of how Antigonus was beheaded. However, he has two different accounts of why this happened. The first version is that Herod feared that Antigonus would be taken to Rome to plead his case to the Senate, and that perhaps they would make one of his sons king. Thus, Herod bribed Antony to have Antigones slain:

> Out of Herod's fear of this it was that he, by giving Antony a great deal of money, endeavored to persuade him to have Antigonus slain, which if it were once done, he should be free from that fear.[167]

The other version comes from Strabo, according to Josephus:

> Now when Antony had received Antigonus as his captive, he determined to keep him against his triumph; but when he heard that the nation grew seditious, and that, out of their hatred to Herod, they continued to bear goodwill to Antigonus, he resolved to behead him at Antioch, for otherwise the Jews could no way be

---

[167] Josephus (*Antiquities of the Jews*), Book XIV, Chapter 16:4.

brought to be quiet. And Strabo of Cappadocia attests to what I have said, when he thus speaks: "Antony ordered Antigonus the Jew to be brought to Antioch, and there to be beheaded. And this Antony seems to me to have been the very first man who beheaded a king, as supposing he could no other way bend the minds of the Jews so as to receive Herod, whom he had made king in his stead; for by no torments could they be forced to call him king, so great a fondness they had for their former king; so he thought that this dishonorable death would diminish the value they had for Antigonus's memory, and at the same time would diminish the hatred they bare to Herod." Thus far Strabo.[168]

These two versions are not necessarily contradictory, since Antony could have had two reasons to behead Antigonus. However, we learn two things: Strabo did have information concerning Herod, even if it is lost to us today. Further, we see that there is no information as to when Antigonus was beheaded. It is likely that some months, at least, passed while Antigonus was Antony's captive. These months would have been sufficient for Herod to start fearing what would happen if Antigonus were brought to Rome, and for Antony to change his mind about keeping Antigonus as a captive, and decide instead to have him beheaded.

It is a problem for us that the death of Antigonus is not dated. According to Josephus, Herod's regnal years are calculated in two ways: from the date the Senate appointed him to be king, and from the date "since he had procured Antigonus to be slain".[169] It is quite clear from Josephus' account that Antigonus had not been sent away from Jerusalem in order to be slain. It would have taken some time for Antigonus to travel to Antioch and some time for Herod

---
[168] Josephus (*Antiquities of the Jews*), Book XV, Chapter 1:2.
[169] Josephus (*Antiquities of the Jews*), Book XVII, Chapter 8:1.

and Mark Anthony to discuss Antigonus' fate. Thus it is reasonable to believe that Antigonus lived some months after the fall of Jerusalem. Those who calculate Herod's reign from the fall of Jerusalem are doing so contrary to Josephus' claims. Further, while it is clear that he must have lived some months, we cannot exclude that he actually sat in prison longer than that, even some years.

However, Josephus also contradicts his own quote from Strabo; according to Strabo, Herod was already officially king before Antigonus was killed, even if the people had not accepted it.

But we should evaluate what Josephus wrote once again, as perhaps the slaying of Antigonus had no connection with Herod's ascension to the throne. Josephus states only that Herod died thirty-four years after having Antigonus slain. Herod might still have counted his regin from the fall of Jerusalem. Conquering Jerusalem would be a better candidate for a starting point to his reign than the death of Antigonus, since Antigonus is obviously beaten and dethroned at that time.

The date 37 BC has been questioned because the ancient historian Cassius Dio reports that in 37 BC "the Romans accomplished nothing worthy of note" in the area.[170] This is interesting, but what does "worthy of note" mean? The objective of the Romans was to fight the Parthians. Was the fall of Jerusalem perhaps simply not a "worthy" Roman accomplishment?

We could use Cassius Dio to attempt to prove that Josephus was wrong in his calculations, as Hutchinson does. However, this book is of the opinion that Josephus based his histories on good sources up until the last decade of Herod's life. In contrast, Cassius Dio wrote more than two hundred years later, and his account therefore ought not to be taken as proof that the Romans did not accomplish anything at all in this area in 37 BC.

---

[170] Cassius Dio (*Roman History*), Book 49.23.1–2.

9.5.3 The Battle of Actium in 31 BC

The next Olympiad that Josephus associates with Herod is the 187th (32–28 BC), when Augustus and Mark Antony fought at the Battle of Actium on 2nd September 31 BC. According to the Attic way of calculating Olympiads, this would have happened in the second year of the 187th Olympiad; but according to the Macedonian way of calculating Olympiads, the battle was fought the first year of the 187th Olympiad. Some months after this battle Herod met Augustus, at this time still known as Octavius.

> The battle at Actium was now expected, which fell into the hundred eighty and seventh olympiad, where Caesar and Antony were to fight for the supreme power of the world. ... At this time it was that the fight happened at Actium, between Octavius Caesar and Antony, in the seventh year of the reign of Herod. [171]

The battle should have happened in Herod's seventh year. Is this possible? What method of counting should we use? Let us start with the Egyptian system, where the first regnal year starts in the preferred calendar year. If we count from the fall of Jerusalem to Herod in 37 BC and use inclusive counting, the seventh year of his reign will be 31 BC. This fits all possible calendars, including the Attic calendar. Even if we use the Macedonian system of counting regnal years, which counts from the specific date of the ascension to the throne, the seventh regnal year will start on 23rd Siwan 38/37 BC, so this also works.

However, we have already seen that Josephus might have counted the regnal years from the death of Antigonus. In such a case, the Attic calendar will probably not work, since some months must have passed between the fall of Jerusalem and the beheading of Antigonus.

---

[171] Josephus (*Antiquities of the Jews*), Book XV, Chapter 5:1–2.

Only if we use inclusive counting and count from the fall of Jerusalem can the seventh regnal year in Josephus be correct.

9.5.4 Herod meets Augustus in 20 BC

The next regnal year that Josephus mentions with respect to Herod is the seventeenth year of his reign, which can be checked against other known facts:

> Now when Herod had already reigned seventeen years, Caesar came into Syria ...[172]

Caesar in this case is Emperor Augustus, and the trip to Syria is known to have occurred early in the summer of 20 BC.[173] Unfortunately, we cannot tell if he arrived in Syria before or after the start of the new Attic year in late June. No Olympiad is mentioned in connection with this event.

The words "had already reigned" are a bit difficult to interpret. Do they mean that we are now in the eighteenth year, or could it be that the seventeenth year has not quite ended? The expression is used twice in *Antiquities of the Jews*, and in the other instance "had already reigned" concerns the ten years of peace under king Asa of Judah, mentioned in the Bible.[174] In this case, it refers to ten completed years. Thus, we should assume that the year intended is the eighteenth, if we count years according to the Egyptian system. This fits well with any calendar that might have been used.

If Augustus arrived in Syria after the anniversary of the fall of Jerusalem to Herod, we would be in the eighteenth year. If we assume that the regnal years were counted from the beheading of Antigonus, the it would not have been the eighteenth year. The reason for this is that Augustus came early in the summer and Antigonus must have lived to the later part of the summer.

---

[172] Josephus (*Antiquities of the Jews*), Book XV, Chapter 10:3.
[173] Rose (2005).
[174] The Bible (MEV), 2 Chronicles 14:1.

9.5.5 The completion of Caesarea

The next Olympiad mentioned by Josephus is the 192nd (12–8 BC). This is said to be the twenty-eighth year of Herod's reign, the year he completed the building works in Caesarea.

> The entire building being accomplished: in the tenth year [from when the construction work started], the solemnity of it fell into the twenty-eighth year of Herod's reign, and into the hundred and ninety-second olympiad. There was accordingly a great festival and most sumptuous preparations made presently, in order to its dedication; for he had appointed a contention in music, and games to be performed naked. He had also gotten ready a great number of those that fight single combats, and of beasts for the like purpose; horse races also, and the most chargeable of such sports and shows as used to be exhibited at Rome, and in other places. He consecrated this combat to Caesar, and ordered it to be celebrated every fifth year.[175]

If we assume that the regnal years were counted from the fall of Jerusalem, the year of the completion of Caesarea would be 11/10 BC. In this case, Josephus does not mention consuls or anything else that might give us a clue as to which year it was. We know that Herod Agrippa died in AD 44 during a festival in Caesarea,[176] but we cannot tell if this was the same festival as the one that King Herod inaugurated; if it was, we would know that the calculation of 11/10 BC would be wrong. However, Caesarea was used for many games, so we cannot know either way, and these dates cannot be said to contradict each other.

---

[175] Josephus (*Antiquities of the Jews*), Book XVI, Chapter 5:1.
[176] Josephus (*Antiquities of the Jews*), Book XIX, Chapter 8:2.

9.5.6 The death of Herod

Josephus tells us that Herod died some time shortly before Passover, after having reigned for thirty-four or thirty-seven years, depending on the start date:

> When he had done these things, he died, the fifth day after he had caused Antipater to be slain; having reigned, since he had procured Antigonus to be slain, thirty-four years; but since he had been declared king by the Romans, thirty-seven.[177]

Josephus has no other date for the death than the mentioned regnal years. In Chapter 9.4.1 we saw that Josephus counts a reign from the date of ascension to the throne to the death of the monarch. Since Herod was appointed to be king in the autumn of 40 BC and became king in the summer of 37 BC, and Antipater was killed at some unknown time after that, the conclusion is that Herod could have died at the earliest in the autumn of 3 BC. Since he should have died in the winter before Passover, the year must be 2 BC, otherwise the thirty-seven and thirty-four years would not have passed. As we saw above, Josephus calculates years in reign from date to date, thus the valid calculation is 40 minus 37 years. If someone does not agree with this and claim that Josephus on this very occasion does not calculate completed years, well then we will end up with the earliest death date in the autumn of 4 BC, but since the death happened shortly before Passover, the death year must be 3 BC. The only mathematical way to harmonize 37 years with a death date in 4 BC is if we assume that Herod was appointed king be the Senate very early in 40 BC and if Josephus on this very occasion did not calculate completed years. This is, as we have seen, historically impossible.

However, it is quite clear that Josephus believed that Herod died before Passover in 4 BC, as we will see below, when we examine his dates for Herod's heirs. Since he dates the death to the first half of

---

[177] Josephus (*Antiquities of the Jews*), Book XVII, Chapter 8:1.

the year, the death would fall before the start of the Attic as well as the Macedonian new year. Consequently, all the dates late in the autumn would fall one year too late according to Josephus, since they occurred after the start of the new year. So if the sources said that something happened in the first year of a certain Olympiad, Josephus would see it as having happened in the last year of the previous Olympiad.

Since it would be strange for Nicolaus of Damascus to cripple his own dates by omitting the year within the Olympiad, it is more likely that Josephus has deliberately crippled the dates to fit his own calculations, and he had to, because he misunderstood when Herod was appointed king by the Senate.

Another example of how Josephus treats dates is his description of Herod's age at the time of his death. In his first book, *The Wars of the Jews*, Josephus states that Herod was seventy years old shortly before he died.[178] In his second book, *Antiquities of the Jews*, he claims that Herod was fifteen years old in the year 47 BC, when he became governor of Galilee. If this were the case then Herod would have died in AD 8, which is quite impossible, since the Romans took over the country in AD 6. Commentators believe that the reference to his being fifteen was a mistake, and that Herod was actually twenty-five years old in 47 BC.[179] In this case, Herod must have died in 2 BC or 1 BC.

In his second book, Josephus removes the reference to Herod's age at the time of his death. Could this be an indication that he realised that the age of seventy was not compatible with Herod dying in 4 BC?

---

[178] Josephus (*The Wars of the Jews*), Book I, Chapter 33:1.
[179] Josephus (*Antiquities of the Jews*), Book XIV, Chapter 9:1.

9.5.7 Herod's heirs

Two of Herod's heirs are of particular interest, since Josephus mentions how long they reigned, and their deaths might be correlated to general Roman history. Using their regnal years, we ought to be able to calculate when they ascended their thrones, provided that Herod did not put them in office and practice coregency. The heirs of most interest are Philip and Archelaus. This is what Jospehus says about Philip:

> About this time it was that Philip, Herod's [that is, Archelaus's] brother, departed this life, in the twentieth year of the reign of Tiberius, after he had been tetrarch of Trachonitis and Gaulonitis, and of the nation of the Bataneans also, thirty-seven years.[180]

Herod in this case is Archelaus (also known as Herod Archelaus), and Philip is Philip the Tetrarch; both were sons of King Herod. According to Josephus, Emperor Augustus granted Archelaus, Antipas and Philip one part each of King Herod's kingdom, which they ruled as ethnarchs. Tiberius' twentieth year was AD 33, and thirty-seven years before this gives us the year 4 BC as the start of Philip's reign.

Regarding Archelaus, Josephus tells us in *The Wars of the Jews* that he ruled up to his ninth year:

> And now Archelaus took possession of his ethnarchy, and used not the Jews only, but the Samaritans also, barbarously; and this out of his resentment of their old quarrels with him. Whereupon they both of them sent ambassadors against him to Caesar; and in the ninth year of his government he was banished to Vienna, a city of Gaul, and his effects were put into Caesar's treasury. But the report goes, that before he was sent

---

[180] Josephus (*Antiquities of the Jews*), Book XVIII, Chapter 4:6.

for by Caesar, he seemed to see nine ears of corn, full and large, but devoured by oxen. When, therefore, he had sent for the diviners, and some of the Chaldeans, and inquired of them what they thought it portended; and when one of them had one interpretation, and another had another, Simon, one of the sect of Essenes, said that he thought the ears of corn denoted years, and the oxen denoted a mutation of things, because by their ploughing they made an alteration of the country. That therefore he should reign as many years as there were ears of corn; and after he had passed through various alterations of fortune, should die. Now five days after Archelaus had heard this interpretation he was called to his trial.[181]

However, in *Antiquities of the Jews*, written about two decades later, the same story is told, but with the number of corns increased to ten. Accordingly, Josephus now tells us that Archelaus ruled up to his tenth year:

But in the tenth year of Archelaus's government, both his brethren, and the principal men of Judea and Samaria, not being able to bear his barbarous and tyrannical usage of them, accused him before Caesar … he related this dream to his friends: that he saw ears of corn, in number ten, full of wheat, perfectly ripe, which ears, as it seemed to him, were devoured by oxen.[182]

Here we can see how Josephus appears to have corrected his text to make it more coherent, as it seems highly unlikely that he is quoting contradictory sources in both of these texts. We do not know for certain why he increased the number of years in the later book, but he probably realised that the ninth year would be one year too little

---

[181] Josephus (*The Wars of the Jews*), Book II, Chapter 7:3.
[182] Josephus (*Antiquities of the Jews*), Book XVII, Chapter 13:2–3.

if it was true that Herod died before Passover in 4 BC, as he claimed. If Archelaus was dethroned in his tenth year, his reign would have started in the spring of 4 BC, which fits in with Josephus' claim about Herod's death.

According to Josephus' account, the taxation process was finished in "the thirty-seventh year of Caesar's victory over Antony at Actium",[183] which was AD 6.

The question must be raised then: did he change any of his other dates in order to make his accounts more coherent?

Let us move on to Herod's other heir, Philip. Josephus claims that Philip had thirty-seven regnal years, but did he calculate this himself or did he find the number in one of his sources? The death of Philip is actually not in the correct chronological order in Josephus' text. Prior to the death of Philip, we read about the governor of Syria, Vitellius. He ordered Pontius Pilate to travel to Rome to meet Tiberius. Pilate did so, but arrived too late, since Tiberius was already dead. This was in AD 37.

If Josephus was correct about the order of events and if thirty-seven years was the correct number of regnal years for Philip, he should have ascended the throne in 1 BC or AD 1. Alternatively, he might have reigned longer than previously assumed; we only know that Philip's territory was handed over to Herod Agrippa after the death of Tiberius. Unfortunately, if we do not trust Josephus, we cannot tell when Philip died.

Thus, even if Josephus' dates point to 4 BC as the year of Herod's death, this will still not be proof that he died that year. It will only prove that Josephus believed him to have died then.

What we have seen here suggests that Josephus has been doing some calculations, and he trusts his own calculations more than the original source. This demonstrates that Josephus is prepared to

---

[183] Josephus (*Antiquities of the Jews*), Book XVIII, Chapter 2:1.

change his information to make it mathematically correct; in short, he feels he has the right to alter information that has been handed down to him – an attitude that unfortunately makes him less reliable.

Josephus' calculations show that he thought Herod died in early 4 BC. This calculation is historically impossible. It rests on the assumption that the Roman Senate made Herod king in early 40 BC. However, we know from historical accounts that this in fact happened in the autumn of 40 BC, and that he died a few months before Passover. This might seem to be a small difference, but this correction moves Herod's death and the start year for his sons' reigns to 2 BC. This means that all Josephus' dates concerning the length of these reigns will fail accordingly, since they rest on the assumption that Herod died in early 4 BC.

Since his dates are correct before the death of Herod, when Josephus rests his account on Nicolaus of Damascus and Strabo, we must assume that from the death of Herod, when Josephus could no longer use these sources, his account is considerably less reliable. The fact that his dates only work if Herod died in early 4 BC does not prove that this date is correct; it only makes it likely that Josephus has been doing some calculations of his own. However, before we dismiss this date completely, we first must examine what other evidence there may be to support it.

9.5.8 The case for 4 BC as the year of Herod's death

The strongest case for believing 4 BC to be the year of Herod's death is that there are coins of Herod's son Antipas that are dated with the regnal year 43. Since the Roman Emperor Caligula dethroned him in AD 39, Antipas could only have reached his forty-third regnal year if he had started his reign in 4 BC or earlier. This seems to be very strong evidence!

However, some authors have proposed that Herod practised coregency with another son, Antipater.[184] This is very likely, since Josephus actually states that Herod's son Antipater governed together with King Herod:

> However, he governed the nation jointly with his father, being indeed no other than a king already.[185]

Antipater got into trouble when he was accused of poisoning Herod's brother Pheroras, the tetrarch of Perea. After torturing several people, Herod found out that the poison had been meant for him; at least, this is what Josephus tells us that Herod believed to be the case. Because of this, Antipater was sentenced to death. He was put in prison and later killed, five days before Herod himself died. We do not know how long he was imprisoned before he was killed, but during this time Herod managed to twice change his will regarding the inheritance of his kingdom.

In the first new will Antipas was to became the heir to the throne. It is quite clear from Josephus' text that Herod kept himself at home, due to his illness. It is thus likely that Antipas already exercised royal power, perhaps as a coregent, in which case the start of his reign would not have coincided with the time of Herod's death. On his deathbed, Herod changed his will again, and Archelaus was appointed to become the new king of the whole area, while his brothers Antipas and Philip would be ethnarcs. Antipas contested this new will before Augustus, but Augustus followed Herod's wishes. However, Herod had made Antipas tetrarch of Perea and Galilee, and Augustus agreed to that. If Antipas was coregent with Herod, it is quite possible that Antipas started counting his regnal years from the time he first began to rule.

---

[184] In fact, prior to Antipater, three sons were given royal dignity by Herod, to be three separate kings within Herod's kingdom. He later strangled two of them and disinherited the third. Josephus (*The Wars of the Jews*), Book I, Chapter 23:5.
[185] Josephus (*Antiquities of the Jews*), Book XVIII, Chapter 1:1.

Since Antipas was the last of Herod's sons to rule, and since Josephus would have known about his coins, he could easily have reached the conclusion that Antipas had begun his reign in 4 BC at the same time as King Herod's death. Alternatively, one of Josephus' sources might have drawn this conclusion and passed it on to him. If Josephus knew that King Herod had died shortly before Passover, he would have regarded the year 4 BC as the actual date when the sons began their reigns. So when he wrote his historical accounts, he might have changed the dates accordingly, since he thought he had this first-hand knowledge.

The fact that Josephus removed the age of Herod at the time of his death further strengthens the assumption that he chose between several different pieces of information that pointed in different directions. Therefore, to see Josephus as just a mechanical secretary making notes of what happened would be a mistake.

To round this discussion of we shall examine another very weak argument for 4 BC as the date of Herod's death, used by some persons. The line of reasoning is that Antipas and Philip named two different cities Julias, according to Josephus. In the case of Antipas, the city was said to have been named after Julia, the name that Augustus' wife, Livia, was given after the death of Augustus in AD 14. According to Josephus, Philip named his city "by the name of Julias, the same name with Ceasar's daughter".[186] Since the daughter Julia was banished in 2 BC, it would not be politically possible to name a city after her after the banishment. Hence, the cities must have been named 2 BC or earlier, and thus the sons must have inherited their father 2 BC or earlier, it is argued, However, from the context, we learn that both the cities were named after the death of Augustus – thus both of them were surely named after Julia, the wife of Augustus. While it is true that the name is also the name of Augustus' daughter, this means nothing given the context.

---

[186] Josephus (*Antiquities of the Jews*), Book XVIII, Chapter 2:1.

Again, Josephus is writing about a time prior to his own and he probably has no other source than the family traditions he mentions. The naming of the cities therefore does not work as evidence that the sons started their reign 4 BC. The only thing we know is that Antipas considered his reign to have started then.

9.5.9 Conclusion

An examination of the dates used in *Antiquities of the Jews* reveals that the dates and regnal years for Herod, prior to his death, are correct, if we assume that these regnal years were counted according to a Jewish or Macedonian calendar. Strabo, as well as Nicolaus of Damascus, could have been behind this, but the later dates must have come from Nicolaus.

The way the dates are written makes it clear that the year of Herod's death must have been 2 BC, if we accept what Josephus has written. However, it is also clear that he himself believed that Herod died in 4 BC. Thus, the dating in *Antiquities of the Jews* cannot be trusted.

The fact that the Olympiad dates have been crippled by removing the specification of the year within the Olympiad, could be seen as a sign that Josephus was aware that his own dates did not correspond with the dates in his sources.

If there was indeed an eclipse close to the time of Herod's death, as Josephus claims, the only possible one was the eclipse in January 1 BC. The eclipse prior to this date occurred in early 4 BC, but we have seen that Herod could not have died at this time if Josephus' regnal years are correct.

The regnal years for Antipas could have begun in 4 BC due to the coregency of Herod and Antipas. In the case of coregency, the counting of regnal years would begin with the start of the co-reign and continue on into the sole reign thereafter.

Josephus tells us that Herod was seventy years old at the time of his death. We have reason to believe that his original source is likely to have said that Herod was twenty-five years old in the year 47 BC. However, we have poor evidence to support the claim that he was seventy years old when he died, since this information seems to have been received only through oral tradition in Josephus' family. However, if this information is correct, we have another reason to believe that Herod died in 2 or 1 BC.

In other words, we cannot be certain when Herod died. Josephus is not a neutral recorder of facts; he makes his own calculations then makes his story fit with those calculations. The number of dates he provides does not prove that Herod died in 4 BC; it only proves that Josephus thought that he did. However, Josephus' calculations collapse, since they are incompatible with history, which produces a date of 2 BC as the year of Herod's death, according to Josephus' own way of counting. Because of this, his calculations for the sons' regnal years will also fail accordingly.

The only external evidence available to us are Antipas' coins, and we have reason to believe that he co-reigned with his father, thus the coins cannot be taken as proof as to when Herod died. The reigns of the other sons could be explained as Josephus' calculations.

Some problems remain. The governor of Syria, Varus, had to intervene militarily in Judah after the death of Herod. He is known to have been governor until 4 BC; after that, we do not know if he or someone else was governor. However, to assume that he was not governor after that point is an argument from silence, and thus a very poor argument. Since Josephus does not seem to have any written sources about this, his information about Varus is not very reliable, thus the name of the governor need not be correct.

9.6 Quirinius and the tax registration

A taxation was held as soon as Archelaus was deposed; that is, in AD 6. In this year, Quirinius became the governor of Syria. Most people therefore assume that Luke's statement about Quirinius being governor when Christ was born is false. Some maintain that Quirinius might have been governor twice, but this is only a guess, which does not form a good basis for conclusions.

Others point to the fact that the Greek Bible does not say that Quirinius was governor. It is only the Roman translation of the Bible that says that Quirinius was governor. The Greek word used in the Bible is ἡγεμών, which means *the one who goes first, guide, leader, chief, governor, prince,* and *ruler.* It is actually the same word used for the Star of Bethlehem, as it leads the magi to Bethlehem. Thus, we must examine if another kind of leadership was intended.

The word "leader" means a leader in general and is etymologically related to the word meaning military leader. Quirinius had led Roman armies in a war in Syria in the last few years of the first century BC. This war occurred not in present-day Syria, but in the Turkish parts of what was once the Roman province of Syria. Quirinius was an honoured military leader after his triumph in this war.[187]

If we assume that Luke is referring to Quirinius more generally as a military leader, or perhaps as having special authority in Syria, this could well fit into the historical picture.

The taxation in AD 6 was the first direct taxation by the Roman government, and it subsequently caused a lot of turmoil. The tax registration mentioned by Luke might have been a completely different event to the taxation in AD 6, an event that would not create the same turmoil as a direct tax paid to the Romans. It is thought by some that Mary and Joseph went to Bethlehem to become registered in advance of taxation, as part of a general taxation registration process that Augustus was conducting to document his empire.[188]

---

[187] See https://en.wikipedia.org/wiki/Quirinius.
[188] Hutchinson (2015), p. 23.

Another view is that Herod would not have been obliged to conduct such a registration, since Judah was in theory a kingship outside Rome. But some claim that Herod would have been forced to conduct a registration because he had angered Augustus and lost his status as Augustus' friend some years earlier (see Chapter 4.8).

I any case, it is not clear that Luke intended that Quirinius was governor and an alternative tax registration, at the same time as Quirinius was conducting war in Syria, could be intended.

9.7 A critical view

Adair is critical of the tendency to change history in order to prove the historicity of biblical text. He would probably argue that the things written above, about Herod's death and the taxation, are just examples of rewriting history to fit the Bible.[189] Adair's warning shall be taken seriously and we should be cautious not to change facts to fit our presumptions and theories. However, Adair is not aware that the dates he uses are not as well established as he thinks. His dates are what most scholars currently believe to be the best available dates, but this does not mean that they are correct.

We have seen above that Josephus seems to have calculated the death date of Herod, and his calculations could rest solely on the length of Antipas reign, who could have co-reigned with Herod.

9.8 Conclusion

A moderate view might be that the stories of Matthew and Luke are true in their broad outline but that certain details, which are not so relevant in the overall picture, are wrong. In reality, the uncertainties are such that different people will draw different conclusions, and people will have a tendency to focus on those details that support their own beliefs.

---

[189] Adair (2013), pp. 11–17.

Some will certainly argue with this book's conclusions concerning the date of Herod's death. All the dates coming from his sources in fact appear to be correct and compatible with historical accounts. However, Josephus' own calculations fail. We must therefore ask: why should we prefer Josephus' calculations when they are not compatible with history? They are clearly nothing but calculations that he tried to make internally consistent, without knowing that they were incompatible with historical fact. And why should we focus on Josephus' account of Herod's death, when he himself seems to indicate that he does not base this account on any written source?

A reader who still wants to maintain that Herod died in 4 BC, 37 years after having been appointed king by the Senate should contemplate the basic mathematical consequences. The measures taken to prove that Herod died after 37 years will destroy the earlier dates for Herod. The reader must contemplate, what is most likely to be correct: dates coming from the eyewitness Nicolaus in accordance with history or dates coming from oral tradition that contradicts history.

Critics will argue that Josephus had no intention of obscuring facts when it came to his statements about the years that someone had ruled. This is true. However, Josephus was born decades later, and obviously gathered data from many different sources. He certainly did his best, but he assumed that his sources needed something of a makeover, such as in the case of Archelaus's dream (see Chapter 9.5.7).

If the basic theory in this book is true, that the magi came from Babylon and that their interpretation of omens in the night sky is preserved in Revelation, then we have clear evidence that the Christian Church could preserve facts. If this is the case, then why should this ability to preserve facts be limited to knowledge of what the magi said and did? Would it not be natural that the name of the king was also preserved in the tradition? If the basic theory is correct, we have every reason to believe that the Christians were able to keep track of who ruled in the country when the magi arrived. The story about the star serves as an historical record if it can be made plausible that the magi actually travelled from Babylon to Bethlehem.

10 The Gospel of John and the Book of Revelation

The ancient Church considered the author of Revelation to be John the Evangelist or John the Presbyter. Some have suggested that they are the same person. Both of them are thought to have been active in Ephesus. According to tradition, Ephesus is also the place to which John brought Mary, the mother of Christ. Based on this tradition, we have no difficulties finding a connection between Mary and John the Presbyter, and thus we can explain how John the Presbyter came to learn about the story of the Star of Bethlehem.

10.1 What do we know about John the Presbyter?

From Revelation, we learn that John the Presbyter believed in Christ as the saviour from sins, and as the Son of God. John the Presbyter was a devout Christian. His interests lay in the signs in the night sky, visions, and in the Old Testament books of Ezekiel and Daniel. He was also very interested in Babylonia. In Revelation 13, he describes a mysterious creature, similar to creatures seen common in Babylonian temple art:

> The beast which I saw was like a leopard. His feet were like those of a bear, and his mouth like the mouth of a lion.[190]

He was well educated about Babylonian matters; for instance, he knew that Babel was connected to harlots. He rightly describes Ezekiel's four creatures with four faces each, as four creatures with

---

[190] The Bible (MEV), Revelation 13:2.

one face each. He also has a tendency to describe things in heaven as if they were stars and planets (see Chapter 6).

When he includes but disguises the story of the Star of Bethlehem in Revelation 12, he disguises the constellations, stars and planets. Mercury is concealed by saying that the seven-headed dragon is red and has crowns. This is in full accordance with Enuma Anu Enlil, and can be easily understood by anyone who has read the manual. Venus and the Virgin are concealed as "a woman", and the Lion is made into a crown or headdress.

10.2 Was John the Presbyter a Babylonian? Was he a magus?

From what has already been said above, it would be easy to conclude that John the Presbyter was a person from Mesopotamia. The Jews in Mesopotamia experienced hard times and persecutions in the first century AD. It is not impossible that a Jew from Babylon would end up in Ephesus.

However, the fact that he seems to be an educated man makes it less necessary to place him in Babylonia. His strong interest in Ezekiel and Daniel suggests that he is interested in studying Babylonia in any way he can. Such an interest would be quite natural if he had heard a story about Babylonian magi visiting Christ in Bethlehem.

A Christian reader would say that John the Presbyter had heard about what the magi saw. The magi interpreted it in terms of their own religion, but John the Presbyter interpreted it in a Jewish/Christian way. Instead of seeing the seven-headed dragon/serpent as the king of Parthia, as the magi did, John the Presbyter saw it as the Devil himself.

A critical reader would not agree fully with the Christian interpretation, and might say that John the Presbyter reduces the importance of Christ by including a fight between a dragon and angels. To a critical reader, this could be seen as evidence that John the Presbyter thought the fight was real, and this is also how the Church has seen it, even if some would maintain that the dragon is just a symbol for the Devil

Another way of seeing it is that the Jews at this time believed in fallen angels, and also that the Devil accused people in front of God. The victory of Christ at the cross, however, meant that the Devil had been beaten, so he could not remain in heaven. Seen in this way, it would suit John the Presbyter to present the fight as a real fight where the Devil was physically thrown out of Heaven. Perhaps he really did see it this way, even if he thought that Mercury and the Hydra were involved. Revelation 12 states: "A great sign appeared in heaven";[191] if the sign were real, then the fight would have to be real too, at least that is how John the Presbyter might have looked at it

Further, a critical scholar would notice that John the Presbyter in no way relates his text to Enuma Anu Enlil in the rest of Revelation. Thus, it seems unlikely that he used it or found it important. To conclude that John the Presbyter was from Babylonia and was familiar with Enuma Anu Enlil seems unnecessary. It is sufficient to assume that he was given the interpretation that the magi gave to Mary and Joseph.

10.3 John the Evangelist

John the Evangelist chose to write his gospel in a completely different way to the other evangelists. His book is not a narrative about Christ; it is a theological explanation of Christ's past, his mission and his divinity. Some maintain that John the Evangelist was influenced by Platonic philosophy.

Studies of the vocabulary in Revelation and the Gospel of John suggest that the vocabulary is somewhat different. However, others

---

[191] The Bible (MEV), Revelation 12:1.

have maintained that the vocabulary is largely the same, and the differences can be explained by the different subjects being discussed. The internal connections between the texts suggest that they are related.[192]

Further, Revelation has some grammatical errors, while the gospel does not. This could suggest that the authors were two different people. Then again, John is traditionally thought to have written Revelation but dictated the gospel, which would explain why the grammatical errors were corrected. Another argument for the two texts to have been written by the same person is that Irenaeus of Lyon only knew one John, and his close connection to Ephesus would have made it likely that he would have had the correct information: that is, that there was only one John.[193]

10.4 John the Evangelist and Ezekiel

On the surface, John the Evangelist seems to lack John the Presbyter's interest in Ezekiel. However, this is a premature conclusion. In Brian Neil Peterson's book *John's Use of Ezekiel*, he shows how the gospel is actually firmly connected to Ezekiel.[194]

Peterson explains how the different episodes in the other gospels have been reorganised in John's gospel in such a way that they correspond with the order of events in Ezekiel. It is not possible to make a simple list comparing the gospel with Ezekiel, since such a list would not do Peterson's work justice. But it is sufficient to say that both Ezekiel and John begin with God in the sky hovering over earth. Next, the books are concerned with how the temple in Jerusalem has been defiled. Later, Ezekiel and the people lack bread; in the same order, Christ gives bread to the people. Ezekiel loses his wife, but is not allowed to mourn. Christ loses Lazarus, and mourns. This list can be significantly lengthened, showing that the

---
[192] Thomas (1992).
[193] Seventh Day Adventist Bible Commentary (1957), pp. 719–720.
[194] Peterson (2015).

arrangement of the gospel suggests that John the Evangelist was highly interested in Ezekiel, just as John the Presbyter was.[195]

Further, the gospel arranges the story about Christ in such a way that Christ's active time, from when he started to preach to the crucifixion, becomes three and a half years, which is in accordance with the fight in Revelation 12, which lasted 1,260 days.

10.5 Conclusion

This book is not primarily interested in whether or not John the Evangelist and John the Presbyter are the same person. It is sufficient to say that every piece of evidence suggests that the two of them were very close, to the point of being one and the same person. Thus, we have no reason to doubt that the author of Revelation had every chance to get either first-hand information from Mary about the visit of the magi, or second-hand information if John the Presbyter is someone other than John the Evangelist.

Some readers, and perhaps some scholars, will probably think that John was really a Babylonian, or someone who wanted to unite Babylonian beliefs with Christianity. Such readers might notice that Ninurta, who is the representative of Christ in the omen, has many similarities with the Greek god Kronos. Ninurta is responsible for time and the seasons, and can thus be seen as the alpha and omega of the year, just as Christ is alpha and omega, the beginning and the end. Ninurta is also a healer and saviour from sins, and he is connected with the sun to such an extent that Saturn is sometimes equated with the sun. Thus, Ninurta can be seen as the light of the world. Finally, the symbol of Ninurta is the solar cross, representative of someone acting in the name of the sun or of being the son and heir of the sun. The Assyrian kings used this symbol to state their authority (see Figure 20 on page 175).

---

[195] Peterson (2015).

Since people are intrigued by mysteries, such theories are likely to emerge, and they will be believed by some. Against these theories, it can be said that the solar cross is used around the globe as a symbol for the sun. Therefore, the fact that a people or a religion in one area uses a cross in no way proves that they have borrowed it from somewhere else. Similarities are not the same thing as borrowing. In addition, the Christian cross is not similar either, since it is an execution instrument.

Figure 20. The Assyrian king Ashurnasirpal II with a cross around his neck [196]

Humans are similar around the globe. We are interested in light, and see it as good. We are warmed by the sun and it feels beneficial. Darkness is frightening to us as small children, and we see darkness as dangerous. Thus, it is not surprising that religions tend to connect

---

[196] © Trustees of the British Museum.

to the sun and light, and link evil with dark. Ideas do not have to be borrowed from other people; they do arise in all of us due to our common experience as humans on earth.

If the theory about the Star of Bethlehem in this book is generally accepted, John is likely to be examined closely. In the end, the conclusion of this examination is likely to be that John was an educated person firmly rooted in the Jewish/Christian traditions, and that John the Evangelist and John the Presbyter are either the same person or were extremely close. It is also likely to be claimed that certain concepts he introduces were borrowed from Babylonia.

Against this, it can be said that John had heard about the Star of Bethlehem, and this was the basis for his interest in Ezekiel and Daniel. He refers to the four creatures because they are present in the basic story about the star, and he discovers that they are better presented as having one face each, since that is how they appear in the sky. Finally, his interest in Babylonia makes him stress the fight between good and bad, light and darkness more systematically than the other authors in the New Testament. This fight does not have to be borrowed from Babylonia. It is present in the books John is especially interested in: Ezekiel and Daniel. Moreover, if John had heard what the magi said about a fight in heaven, it is not surprising if he gets interested in the fight between darkness and light.

If the theory in this book is generally accepted, many persons will try prove that Christianity has borrowed from Babylonia. Against this, one firm question must be raised: How can it be that the Christian movement knew about the signs in 3 and 2 BC. To the author of this book, the obvious conclusion is that the magi came to Christ at some point. The magi transferred some ideas, and they happened to be in accordance with the Messianic hopes:

> For unto us a child is born, unto us a son is given, and the government shall be upon his shoulder. And his name shall be called Wonderful Counselor, Mighty

God, Eternal Father, Prince of Peace. 7 Of the increase of his government and peace there shall be no end, upon the throne of David and over his kingdom, to order it and to establish it with justice and with righteousness, from now until forever. The zeal of the Lord of Hosts will perform this.[197]

---

[197] The Bible (MEV), Isaiah 9:6-7

11 Did Luke know about the Star of Bethlehem?

This chapter might not not be very appealing to some Christian readers, as it aims to study the Bible from a critical point of view. Essentially, we will be looking at Luke's story about the angels and shepherds as if it had been invented by Luke. Some readers are quite convinced that all the gospels are fiction, but if the story about the magi is true, how would this influence a critical study of Luke?

Of course, it is possible to believe that the shepherds and the magi received separate messages about the same event, and since God sent this message, the messages will be similar; this would be the Christian point of view. This chapter, however, is about how the story of the Star of Bethlehem might influence critical studies of the Bible.

11.1 Did Luke know about the star?

As we saw in Chapter 3.2.2, the early Christians connected the story of the Star of Bethlehem to the Bible passage: "a star will rise out of Jacob, and a man will spring from Israel" (Numbers 24:17 LXX). This text is from Septuagint, the Greek translation of the Old Testament, which was used by the early Church. In the version used in Christianity today, the passage reads: "a star will come out of Jacob, and a scepter will rise out of Israel".[198] The star was seen as the fulfilment of this prophecy, and it was common among the later kings of Judah to try to present themselves as the fulfilment of this prophecy.

Luke does not refer to Numbers directly. However, in Luke 1 he says:

---

[198] The Bible (MEV), Numbers 24:17.

78 through the tender mercy of our God, whereby the sunrise from on high has visited us; 79 to give light to those who sit in darkness and in the shadow of death, to guide our feet into the way of peace.[199]

Could the "sunrise from on high" be referring to Balaam's star (see Chapter 2.9). If so, it could be an indication that Luke connects the birth of Christ to a new light in the skies. This connection is very weak and not convincing, at least not without the support of further evidence. Another alternative is that Luke is referring to Isaiah 9:

> 2 The people who walked in darkness have seen a great light; those who dwell in the land of the shadow of death, upon them the light has shined… 6 For unto us a child is born, unto us a son is given… [200]

Luke might have known about the star, and seen it as the star of Balaam or as the light in the shadow of death, or perhaps both.

11.2 Did Luke know about the magi?

If Luke knew about the star, which is difficult to prove, he would also probably have heard about the magi. We know that he is the author of Acts, and in Acts he uses the word "magi" to mean "sorcerer" (see Chapter 3.2.1). He was therefore likely to have had a negative attitude towards magi.

If he knew about the star and the magi, he could have excluded them from his gospel and introduced the shepherds instead, it could be argued. The story about the magi and the story about the shepherds can be seen to resemble each other:

- Both stories are about the birth of a saviour
- Both the shepherds and the magi receive the message at night while they are on watch

---

[199] The Bible (MEV), Luke 1:78–79.
[200] The Bible (MEV), Isaiah 9:2

- Both the shepherds and magi look up to the sky when they receive the message, as the angels rise up to heaven after speaking to the shepherds, and the magi see their message in the stars
- Both messages signal peace
- Both the shepherds and the magi travel to seek a child

In Chapter 2.11, we saw that stars and angels could be used interchangeably. The stories thus resemble each other, and the story about the shepherds can be seen as a variant on the same theme: with the help of angels/stars, God reveals that the saviour is born and peace shall come.

The main theory in this book is that Revelation 12 is a description of what the magi saw. We saw that, according to the skies and the omens, the woman went and sought nourishment in her hidden place for 1,260 days. According to Enuma Anu Enlil, this was the sign of peace for Amurru – of reconciliation with the gods (see Chapter 7.6.7). This is in full accordance with Luke's angels saying "Glory to God in the highest heaven, and on earth peace to those on whom his favour rests" in the following passage:

> 9 An angel of the Lord appeared to them, and the glory of the Lord shone around them, and they were terrified. 10 But the angel said to them, "Do not be afraid. I bring you good news that will cause great joy for all the people. 11 Today in the town of David a Savior has been born to you; he is the Messiah, the Lord. 12 This will be a sign to you: You will find a baby wrapped in cloths and lying in a manger." 13 Suddenly a great company of the heavenly host appeared with the angel, praising God and saying, 14 "Glory to God in the highest heaven, and on earth peace to those on whom his favor rests." 15 When the angels had left them and gone into heaven, the shepherds said to one another,

"Let's go to Bethlehem and see this thing that has happened, which the Lord has told us about."[201]

We saw in Chapter 7.6.7 that Venus indicated the birth of the child, and that it would be a difficult birth. We also saw that Venus heralded the moment of the birth and signalled to the magi that peace would come. The movement of Venus, as she leaves Jupiter after having delivered her message, also fits well with the description of the angel going back to heaven after having delivered her message to the shepherds. The expression that the gods will be reconciled with Amurru, as Enuma Anu Enlil says, also fits well with "peace to those on whom his favour rests", as the peace and the favour of the gods is the same thing.

The message from the angels is actually one of the most difficult verses to translate, since it has two versions differentiated by a single letter, the very last letter in the sentence:

ἐπὶ γῆς εἰρήνη ἐν ἀνθρώποις εὐδοκίας

or

ἐπὶ γῆς εἰρήνη ἐν ἀνθρώποις εὐδοκία

The first version is favoured by most scholars today, and is seen as the original version. The word translated as "good will" or "favoured" is in the genitive case, thus it describes something owned or kept. It might reflect a Semitic expression that sounded strange in Greek, and thus the last letter was removed to make it sound better in Greek. A literal translation of each version above would be:

on earth, peace to men [owning or enjoying] good will

or

on earth peace, good will to men

---

[201] The Bible (NIV), Luke 2:9–15.

Peace to men of good will is a limitation on whom the peace is bestowed. However, it reflects the double meaning of the omen about peace/reconciliation for Amurru in Enuma Anu Enlil. A person who is reconciled with the gods is also a person who is at peace. To be reconciled with the gods is to enjoy their good will. When Venus leaves her secret place after 1,260 days, Amurru enjoys the good will of the gods and the period of peace begins – for all those who are reconciled with the gods.

Seen in this way, the story of the shepherds is the same as the story of the magi seeing the star on 17th June 2 BC.

Matthew and Luke are the evangelists who talk about the events surrounding the birth of Christ. Matthew talks about kingship, but not peace. Where did Luke get the idea about a message of peace? A Christian response would be that God sent his angel to the shepherds and told them the same message that the magi could read in the night sky. Another explanation is that Luke was fully aware of the story of the Star of Bethlehem, but chose to transform it into a story about pious shepherds.

From a critical point of view, we should notice that Jupiter standing still was a sign of peace, and Venus hiding in her secret place was also a sign of peace. However, we must remember that neither Matthew nor John ever mentions the word "peace" in relation to these celestial events. From the perspective of a critical analysis, this could serve as an argument for the existence of a common source. This source is in accordance with Enuma Anu Enlil, as has been presented in this book. Matthew, Luke and John have all included this source in different ways in their texts.

This ought to be our conclusion, if these texts are analysed in the same way that other texts are normally analysed. A Christian response would be that God revealed one and the same message in three different ways in the New Testament, and in a fourth way to the magi – and they all completely agree with each other.

11.3 What about the peace?

The Christmas message is said to be about peace on earth – why? Was the early Christian experience that Christ brought peace? And did there turn out to be a new kingdom on earth?

From the perspective of early Christians, Christ did not bring earthly peace or an earthly kingdom; but this is exactly what the angels seemed to think, and it is also exactly what the magi expected the new Alexander the Great to bring. The early Christians talked about Christ as the king of kings and a bringer of peace. This is odd, but understandable if the visit of the magi really happened and influenced the Church as a result.

11.4 Conclusion

We know from Acts 13:6–8 that Luke does not speak favourably about the magi, and even sees them as sorcerers (see Chapter 3.2.2). The story of the shepherds can be seen as Luke's version of the story about the magi, without mentioning them at all. Every obvious connection to the magi, stars and constellations has been removed, but the message is still the same. In this respect, Luke is similar to John the Presbyter, who also told the story in Revelation 12, but masked every clear connection to magi, stars and constellations. In the same way, the Gospel of John tells the story of how the Word of God came down to earth, by referring to Ezekiel but without mentioning magi, stars or constellations (see Chapter 10.5).

Biblical scholars will not be immediately convinced that Luke's story is based on a tradition about the magi from the east telling a story similar to the one in Revelation. Whether this conclusion gains acceptance among critical scholars will depend on how Revelation 12 is perceived. If it is generally accepted that Revelation 12 preserves an account of actual contact between the early Christians and the magi of Babylonia, then Luke's shepherds are likely to be examined more closely.

Since the stories resemble each other and since many scholars do not believe in Christ, they may well assume that Luke invented the story about the shepherds based on the story about the star. The Christian response would be that God gave the same message to the shepherds as he gave to the magi, and this is why the stories are similar.

12 Consistency of the omens

12.1 Why compare omens?

The theory in this book is based on omens. A critical reader might think that such a large number of omens from different times and places must generate a number of alternative readings. Could it be that this book has picked out the fitting omens and omitted the others?

In order to present the material more effectively for a critical reader, this chapter has been written to explain how the omens have been compared, and how the different omens relate to each other.

Today we have no unified edition of Enuma Anu Enlil, and we probably never will, unless a more complete set of tablets is discovered. To compare omens is, thus, a huge task, as we do not have a main set of tablets that could serve as proof to compare with the smaller finds.

In this chapter, the crucial omens that have been discussed will be examined and related to other omens to see whether alternative explanations exist, and if so, how these would affect the theory that the magi wanted to find a new Alexander the Great. These omens will be compared with others in Enuma Anu Enlil, both within the same version, and between different versions.

12.2 Comparison of omens where the event is the same: how consistent are the predictions?

Enuma Anu Enlil has come down to us in perhaps five different versions (see Chapter 2.2). Can we rely on these sources, or can they be used to prove almost anything? How much do the omens differ? These questions are difficult to answer, since the tablets are fragmentary and we have never found a complete version. A better way to examine how the magi would have interpreted a sign is to look at all the available tablets, and present any alternative interpretations.

A sceptical person would say that it is not sufficient to look at one omen and look for alternative interpretations in other versions. Since some omens might be lacking in some versions, it could be that the versions appear to be more consistent than they really are.

A better approach to compare the omens is therefore to look at a group of similar celestial events where the number of omens is high. One such example is where Jupiter is connected to the Scorpion. Several such omens exist, but many of them are damaged; either we can read the condition but not the consequence, or the other way around. However, there are fortunately still plenty of complete omens.

By comparing omens this way, we will be able to tell whether it is likely that the omens are consistent between different versions of Enuma Anu Enlil or whether the omens have been altered and contradict each other. If the latter is true, it would be difficult to say how the magi would have interpreted the omens of importance in this book.

The omens are not numbered or classified in any way, so it is difficult to refer to them. In the list below, the omens are therefore referred to by citing pages in Reiner's book, *Babylonian Planetary Omens*, which contains a translated compilation of all the available omens from all the different versions of Enuma Anu Enlil stone tablets.[202] On each page the omens are described, or sometimes classified as unreadable. In some cases, the omens are very similar to those on another page.

The conditions and predictions relating to Jupiter in the Scorpion are compared below, although they are not presented in detail. The

---

[202] Reiner (2005), pp. 43, 53, 55, 83, 87, 89, 93, 99, 101.

omens are compared to find out if they are contradictory. Readers who are interested in exploring the subject further are encouraged to read Reiner's book.

Page 43. Rules stating what will happen to trade and markets in different areas.

Page 53. Unreadable.

Page 55. Conditions do not match page 43. Predictions are unreadable.

Page 83. Conditions similar to page 55. Seems almost identical to page 55.

Page 87. Identical to page 43.

Page 89. Similar to page 43 but large parts are unreadable.

Page 93. Rules about "weapons" of different countries.

Page 99. Several rules not related to other versions.

Page 101. Similar to page 43.

In the examination above, we find that some editions of the omen series have different conditions and predictions. Page 43 and page 55 seem to be clearly different regarding the order of the omens, so these are certainly different versions. However, if we look at the individual omens, they do not contradict each other, even if the order is completely different.

The rules on page 99 are different from all the other versions, and concern Jupiter (called Sulpae) inside the horn of the Scorpio, or when it has reached the neck of the Scorpion. There are no rules about these conditions in the other tablets. Page 43 and page 55 have only one condition in common; unfortunately the consequence is unreadable on page 43 and on the tablets similar to it.

Page 93 has a rule about Jupiter in the sting of the Scorpion. The consequence differs from page 83, but the rule differs slightly too. Page 83 describes Jupiter standing in the sting while page 93 describes Jupiter reaching the sting. Of course, Jupiter cannot stand in the sting without reaching it in the first place, but we do not know if this means that the rules indicate different traditions – that a standing Jupiter should be interpreted in another way than a normal moving Jupiter. Since the omens say nothing about what to do when two omens follow naturally on from each other, it is likely that all predictions are valid.

The examination reveals that Enuma Anu Enlil is not as strictly ordered as we would like it to be. Perhaps the scribes treated the rules in the same way as we treat proverbs. The order of the proverbs is not important, and we can change this without violating them.

This examination in no way pretends to be a complete examination. With about seven thousand rules, it would be surprising if two rules did not at some point have the same condition and different consequences. By examining how Jupiter in Scorpio is treated in different versions of Enuma Anu Enlil we discovered that the omens resemble each other even if they are in a completely different order. Thus, even if there are at least five versions of Enuma Anu Enlil, the differences mainly concern the order, rather than the contents of the omens.

We have therefore no reason to doubt that the omens found by archaeologists are the same as those that were used when Christ was born.

12.3 Consistency of the omens regarding Venus and Jupiter when both planets appear together

Enuma Anu Enlil is ordered in such a way that omens concerning the moon are in one section, omens concerning Venus are in another section, and omens concerning Jupiter are in a third section. We must now ask ourselves if these omens are in agreement with each other. If Venus and Jupiter are together in one way in the Venus section, is the rule the same in the Jupiter section?

In fact, they are not the same, and the reason is that the omens are consulted according to which planet is the active one. Venus approaching Jupiter is not the same condition as Jupiter approaching Venus.

Thus, there is one rule for Jupiter passing Venus, and another rule for Venus passing Jupiter, but no rule for Venus when it is being passed by Jupiter. The conditions from Jupiter's point of view are best seen on page 41 in *Babylonian Planetary Omens: Part Four*. The conditions begin with Jupiter either approaching, reaching or passing Venus. Alternative readings on other pages of the book are few, and most of them seem to be fragments of what can be found on page 41. For example, the meeting of the two stars means war. If Jupiter passes above Venus, the dynasty of Akkad will fall. An eclipse of Jupiter by Venus, where Jupiter is the approaching planet, means the end of the dynasty of Amurru. If Jupiter passes Venus, that is, if Venus is slower than Jupiter, there will be a weak flood.[203]

The conditions from Venus' point of view are dispersed over several pages. The language used is also a bit different. For instance, the term "crown" is used to describe a star passing an object. The name for Jupiter also varies in different sources. The name is sometimes "Great star" or "Sulpae" instead of the more common Akkadian name "UD.AL.TAR", and these different names can sometimes be used in the same text.

At first glance, the omens for Venus approaching Jupiter seem contradictory, even on the same tablet. Venus coming near to Jupiter and Venus coming close to Jupiter have two different consequences. Should the predictions not be the same? The

---

[203] Reiner (2005), pp. 41, 47, 51, 57, 61, 79, 99, 101.

confusion is solved when we learn how the words "near" and "close" are used as measurements. Coming "near" means to be less than two fingers apart (with an outstretched arm), and coming "close" means less than one finger apart.[204] Thus, we do not actually have different consequences for the same events. On the contrary, we have a list of omens that become worse and worse for Akkad, the closer Venus comes to Jupiter.

The first two rules mean a great flood. In the third rule, Venus reaches Jupiter and passes it, again meaning a flood. The fourth rule, when they come "close", suggests the king of Amurru will have a reign of destruction. In the fifth rule, Venus comes near", and brother will be against brother. In the sixth rule, Venus eclipses or touches Jupiter with the consequence that the king of Akkad will die and the dynasty will change.[205]

Different consequences also occur depending on the situation: floods will arrive when the planets meet, and the character of the floods will depend on which of the two planets is the active and approaching one. Both situations involve floods, under certain circumstances, but if Jupiter is the active planet, the floods will be limited. If Venus is active, the floods will be more devastating.[206]

We now see that an eclipse of Jupiter by Venus has different meanings depending on which planet approaches which. If Jupiter is the approaching planet when Jupiter and Venus come close, the consequence will be the end of the dynasty of Amurru; but if Venus is the approaching planet, the dynasty of Akkad will end.

Thus the fact that there are omens for Jupiter and omens for Venus does not mean that there is a risk of contradictions, since the rules are written in such a way that it is quite clear that what matters is which planet is the approaching one. In the Jupiter section, Jupiter

---

[204] Sachs and Hunger (1998), p. 11.
[205] Reiner and Pingree (1998), p. 45.
[206] Reiner and Pingree (1998), p. 45; Reiner (2005), p. 61.

is the approaching planet and in the Venus section, Venus is the approaching planet.

12.4 Conclusion

After having examined the conditions and consequences, it seems as if Enuma Anu Enlil was kept in good internal order, even if the order of omens seems to have changed in different editions. In relation to the Star of Bethlehem, it seems clear that when Venus passed Jupiter on 17th June 2 BC, it constituted a very rare series of conditions, and the prediction for the magi from this would have been that a king from Amurru would kill the king of Akkad and take the throne.

Anyone observing the events in the night sky in September in 3 BC and in June in 2 BC would therefore have come to approximately the same conclusions in terms of predictions, no matter which version of Enuma Anu Enlil they were consulting.

13 Conclusion

13.1 What is the theory of this book?

The theory is that Revelation 12 is a description of what the magi saw; they interpreted what they saw using their divination manual, Enuma Anu Enlil, and it was this interpretation that brought them to Jerusalem. What they saw was two clear messages that a revolution was going to take place in Mesopotamia. A new king would arrive from Amurru, in the west, and replace the present dynasty. Since the present dynasty was not good for the Babylonians, their culture or their religion, the magi saw this sign as a positive thing.

The two omens were nine months apart and the first omen contained information about a difficult birth. These two pieces of information were included in the main theory, and thus the theory was that a new king had been born somewhere in Amurru. Since Amurru was seen as the area between Mesopotamia and the eastern shores of the Mediterranean Sea, it was natural for them to travel to Jerusalem, where a large population was governed by a semi-independent king, who could perhaps be equated with the father of Alexander the Great, the last king that had been beneficial for Babylon.

This prediction brought the magi to Jerusalem, where they were directed to Bethlehem. As they travelled the road down to Bethlehem in the early morning, they found that the king star, Jupiter, seemed to always be in front of them, since the road to Bethlehem turns gradually to the west in the same way that Jupiter would have done in the mornings in December in 2 BC.

When they arrived, the magi concluded that Jupiter had come to its stationary point, and this was for them a confirmation that they had found their new king. Jupiter standing still in the morning meant, according to Enuma Anu Enlil, that kings would be reconciled and that peace was to come to earth.

Enuma Anu Enlil suggested that a delegation should be sent to the enemy, asking for peace. As a result the magi travelled to Jerusalem, where they were directed towards Bethlehem, and as they arrived in Bethlehem they saw the message about peace on earth.

13.2 What have we studied?

This book has covered a range of subjects. We have travelled back to an era and a culture far away in terms of time and place. We have studied basic astronomy, history and culture from the relevant areas. We are not accustomed to their way of thinking. We have seen that they studied the stars, and we have seen that their divination manual has been covered under sand and soil for more than two millennia, but is now recovered, translated and available to us.

We have not used the manual ourselves, and we are not accustomed to all of the concepts in the manual. Some parts we do not understand and some parts we know to be missing.

Very few people have read this manual, and not many are acquainted with all the information needed to use it, especially since it is a new area of study for most of us. Thus, it is likely that some readers of this book will be reluctant to draw any conclusions. This is a sound strategy. The theory in this book is new, and it has to be reviewed from many different points of view. It also raises new questions, such as: when did the Christians first hear about these celestial events?

It would be vain to believe that this book might fundamentally change people's minds. A Christian reader will remain Christian, and an atheist reader will remain an atheist. With this in mind, the book has tried to deliver different points of view. The atheist will probably dislike some views, and the Christian will probably dislike others. However, it is hopeless to try to anticipate what a reader will think about a text, or to try to cater for many different views.

At best, the book will be read and evaluated by others in different areas of science. Biblical scholars are likely to avoid the subject for a while, until they have learned how experts on Enuma Anu Enlil have assessed it.

A good priest or preacher will also stick to the Word of God when it comes to talking about the visit of the magi. If the theory in the book is true, the early Christians chose not to present it in its full extent, partly because they lived in a syncretistic culture, where some of the members of the Church could try to mix Christianity with other religions. In the same way, we in our time run the same risk of mixing the Word of God with science.

Thus, this book should be read in a contemplative way. The book has some new theories, and it criticises certain other theories. These new theories must be evaluated, and more research is needed. We will now summarise some of its subjects, and point to relevant questions, weaknesses, opportunities and possibilities for further research.

13.3 How should the Star of Bethlehem be examined?

As we have seen throughout the book, the general approach has always been to look at special events in the night sky. However, we have also seen that some of these special events, such as conjunctions of Jupiter and Saturn, are regular. A scholar would have to push such events very far, or perhaps even inflate them, to turn them into a theory about why some magi travelled to Jerusalem.

Some theories do not even contain a trip to Jerusalem. Such theories are just ways of trying to find a special event that might have triggered Christian interest. Such theories have even less of a foundation, as they rest on the assumption that others will complete the picture with mere fantasies to make up for the lack of evidence.

Adair is a total sceptic, which is always refreshing. A critic forces us to ask ourselves what we really know. His demand that a theory should explain all the information in the Bible, including why the magi left for Jerusalem and how the star led them to Bethlehem, is a challenge worth taking on. However, Adair goes too far. No theory can appear fully developed without error, and many of the theories we take for granted today originally had many weaknesses. A good theory is open for revision and is improved by it. Thus, Adair's demand is a good goal to try to reach, but if a theory does not reach all the way, it may still be on the path leading to increased knowledge.

This book strongly advises that Enuma Anu Enlil should be consulted when a theory in this field is tested. We have seen that the Babylonian magi were the main diviners using the stars, and any theory must therefore relate to the magi. This is not the same as saying that all the theories must be in accordance with Enuma Anu Enlil. However, it is a great weakness if a theory does not discuss its relation to Enuma Anu Enlil. We have the ability to test any theory against a relevant divination manual, and this should therefore be done if a theory is to be taken seriously.

This book has combined astronomy, the divination manual and the political and cultural context at the time to establish and support its theory. Time will tell how successful this theory is.

13.4 Is the Bible a necessary reference in a valid theory?

In this book, Revelation 12 is used to demonstrate that a text in the Bible is written in such a way that it can be understood, explained and tested against astronomical events the years 3 BC and 2 BC. This is not the same as saying that the theory is proven, but it does seem to be the best yet. However, who knows what the decipherment of new texts could yield?

A special point of interest is the relation between the Bible and the secret place of Venus (see Chapter 7.6.7). Scholars interested in Enuma Anu Enlil are currently not sure where this secret place is. Its identification in this book rests on one single find. Is this sufficient? Will Revelation 12 be used to finally determine where Venus's secret place was, or will scholars continue to try to connect the secret place with Greek exaltations, even though this method has not been entirely successful in the past?

A connection between the Bible and Enuma Anu Enlil is, of course, a good thing for a theory, but a theory does not need to rest on hidden information in the Bible. If another theory could be found that fits better with Enuma Anu Enlil, such a theory must be taken seriously even if the connection to the Bible is weak.

13.5 What are the consequences for Christianity?

Since Christianity is very diverse, the theory in this book will be taken very differently by different Christian groups. Some will be offended by the idea that the wise men went to find a king to suit their own personal needs, although others will say that this is often the case when people come to God. We do not know how the magi kept in contact with Christ and to what conclusion they eventually came.

Some will criticise Christianity and say that the story about Christ and the wise men is just a Mesopotamian myth that was turned into a messianic religion. However, it would be extremely strange for an early Christian to have gone back in time, found events in the night sky, read a foreign religion's divination manual and then constructed a story based on it, disguised it and then sent it to people who had no chance of understanding what the story meant. It is far simpler to assume that the magi actually went to Christ. A Christian will believe that they went to Bethlehem, while others might believe that the magi met Christ as an adult.

However, if the magi first met Christ as an adult, why did the early Christians not say so? The magi had obviously been studying the night sky in 3 BC and in 2 BC. If they went to Christ thirty or so years later and concluded that he was the intended king, why would the Christians have invented the story about the magi visiting Herod? Is it not more likely that they actually went to Jerusalem and travelled down to Bethlehem on a December morning in 2 BC? Is this not the simplest solution, and the easiest to believe?

In the end, the theory in this book is no threat to Christianity. On the contrary, it makes it likely that the gospels and early Christians truthfully preserved what happened and what they saw.

Some might use this theory to develop the interpretation of Revelation 12. What exactly was the significance behind the woman fleeing to her secret place? The secret place is at the feet of the dragon killer, the constellation Ophiuchus, and according to old theories about the gospel in the skies, this place is called "the place where the dragon killer got stung in the heal", or in other words, Calgary/Golgatha. Thus, the woman is searching for nourishment at Calgary when the dragon is after her.

Some will notice that according to John, Christ's mission on earth ended at Calgary after three and a half years; exactly the same time that the woman sought security in the secret place. Others will say that this is because John knew what the magi saw and wrote his gospel in such a way that it conformed to Enuma Anu Enlil. The Christian response would be to ask: why would he do that, if he then concealed the information so no one would understand it?

13.6 What are the consequences for Biblical science?

As was said at the beginning of this chapter, scholars in the Biblical sciences will be reluctant to study this theory until it has been examined by those who have deeper knowledge about Enuma Anu Enlil. If the theory in this book stands the test, several consequences will follow. The origin of Christianity will be seen in a new light, and some scholars may try to prove that Christianity is the result of a messianic hope based on a Babylonian omen, remade after the unexpected execution of its leader. People who do not believe will always try to build new theories that can prove their point of view. At the same time, Christians will try to defend their belief by similar means.

However, those who have an open mind are the ones who will search, and the ones who search will find. The question is, do we accept what we find or reject it because we do not like the consequences?

To conclude this book, I would like to thank Larson for his theory about the Star of Bethlehem and Revelation 12. He was ready to see the message in the Star without all evidence, and that is what Christianity is about: believing in God, not because of any proof, but because of faith in who God is, and the love He stands for.

> For now we see as through a glass, dimly, but then, face to face. Now I know in part, but then I shall know, even as I also am known. 13 So now abide faith, hope, and love, these three. But the greatest of these is love. [207]

---

[207] The Bible (MEV), 1 Corinthians 13:12-13.

Literature

The Bible

Three translations have been used:

The Bible (MEV), The Holy Bible, Modern English Version. Copyright © 2014 by Military Bible Association. Published and distributed by Charisma House, Florida. All rights reserved. http://modernenglishversion.com/

The Bible (NIV), The Holy Bible, New International Version, NIV Copyright © 1973, 1978, 1984, 2011 by Biblica, Inc. All rights reserved worldwide http://www.biblica.com/bible/

The Bible (Berean), The Holy Bible, Berean Study Bible, BSB Copyright ©2016 by Bible Hub. All Rights Reserved Worldwide. http://bereanbible.com/

Other

Adair, Aaron (2013), "The Star of Bethlehem: A Sceptical View", Lighting Source International,
Bible – "Modern English Version" (MEV), http://modernenglishversion.com/, Charisma House, Florida, 2015

Bagnall, Roger S (2009), "The Oxford Handbook of Papyrology", Oxford University Press, New York

Biltcliffe, D. A. W. (1970), "Nicolaus of Damascus: His Historical Writings, With Particular Reference to his Biography of Augustus", PHD-thesis, University of Leicester

Burgess, Richard W (1999), "Studies in Eusebian and Post-Eusebian Chronography", Franz Steiner Verlag, Stuttgart

Campion, Nicholas (2008), "A History of Western Astrology – Volume I The Ancient World", Bloomsbury Academic (2015), London

Dio, Cassius, "Roman History", in http://penelope.uchicago.edu/Thayer/e/roman/texts/cassius_dio/home.html

Hannah, Darrell D (2015), "The Star of the Magi and the Prophecy of Balaam in Earliest Christianity, with Special Attention to the Lost Books of Balaam", in "The Star of Bethlehem and the Magi", see van Kooten!

Hegedus, Tim (2007), "Early Christianity and Ancient Astrology", Peter Lang Publishing, New York

Hunger, Hermann; Pingree, David (1999), "Astral Sciences in Mesopotamia", Brill, Leiden

Hutchinson, Dwight (2015), "The Lion Led the Way", Edition Signes Celestes, St Paul-Trois-Chateaux

Irenaeus of Lyon, "Against Heresies", in "New Advent", http://www.newadvent.org, which contains Alexander, Roberts; Donaldsson, James; Clevland Coxe A, (1885), "From Ante-Nicene Fathers, Vol 1", Christian Literature Publishing Co, Buffalo

Jenkins, R M (2004), "The Star of Bethlehem and the comet of AD 66", in "Journal of the British Astronomical Association", Vol 114, No. 6, p.336

Josephus Titus Flavius, "Antiquities of the Jews", at https://archive.org/details/theAntiquitiesOfTheJews_507

Josephus Titus Flavius, "War of the Jews", https://archive.org/details/theWarsOfTheJews

Koch, Dieter (2015), "The Star of Bethlehem", Zürich

Koch-Westenholz (1995), "Mesopotamian Astrology – An Introduction to Babylonian and Assyrian Celestial Divination", The Carsten Niebuhr Institute of Near Eastern Studies Museum Tusculanum Press, Copenhagen

Larson, Frederick A, (2017), http://www.bethlehemstar.com/

Lidell, Henry George; Scott, Robert (1996), "Greek-English Lexicon", Oxford University Press, Oxford

Münter, Friedrich (1827), "Der Stern der Weisen: Untersuchungen über das Geburtsjahr Christi", J H Schubothe,

Copenhagen
Ossendrijver, Mathieu (2015), "The Story of the Magi & Encounters with Caldeans", in "The Star of Bethlehem and the Magi", see van Kooten!
Parpola, Simo (2009), "The Magi and the Star – Babylonian astronomy dates Jesus' birth", in "The First Christmas – The story of Jesus' Birth in History and Tradition", edited by Murphy, Sara; Bronder, Robert; Laden, Susan, Biblical Archaeology Society, Washington DC
Peterson, Brian Niel (2012), "Ezekiel in Context – Ezekiel's Message Understood in Its Historical Setting of Covenant Curses and Ancient Near Eastern Mythological Motifs", Pickwick Publications, Eugene, Oregon
Peterson, Brian Niel (2015), "John's Use of Ezekiel – Understanding the Unique Perspective of the Fourth Gospel", Fortress Press, Minneapolis
Polybius, "The Histories" in http://penelope.uchicago.edu/Thayer/E/Roman/Texts/Polybius/home.html
Reiner, Erica, (2005), "Babylonian Planetary Omens – Part Three", Styx Publications, Groningen
Reiner, Erica; Pingree, David (1998), "Babylonian Planetary Omens – Part Four", Brill-Styx, Leiden
Rochberg, Francesca (1998), "Babylonian Horoscopes", American Philosophical Society, Philadelphia
Rochberg, Francesca (2004), "The Heavenly Writing – Divination, Horoscopy, and Astronomy in Mesopotamian Culture", Cambridge University Press (2011), Cambridge
Rochberg, Francesca (2010), "In the Path of the Moon – Babylonian Celestial Divination and Its Legacy", Brill, London
Rose, Charles Brian (2005), "The Parthians in Augustan Rome", in American Journal of Archaeology 109, p. 21-75
Sachs, Abraham J; Hunger, Herman (1988), "Astronomic Diaries and Related Texts From Babylonia", Verlag der

Österreichischen Akademie der Wissenschaft, Wien
Scheck, Thomas P. (2008), "Saint Jerome: Commentary on Matthew" in "The Fathers of the Church, Volume 117)" edited by Halton Thomas P, The Catholic University of America Press, USA
Thiele, Edwin R (1951), "The Mysterious Numbers of the Hebrew Kings", Macmillan, New York
Thomas, Robert L (1992), "Revelation Exegetical Commentary", Moody Publishers, Chicago
van der Waerden, Bartel L; Huber, Peter (1974), "Science Awakening II – The Birth of Astronomy", Springer Science + Business Media, Dordrecht
van Kooten (2015), "Matthew, the Parthians, and the Magi: A Contextualization of Matthew's Gospel in Roman-Parthian Relations of the First Centuries BCE and CE", in "The Star of Bethlehem and the Magi – Interdisciplinary Perspectives from Experts on the Ancient Near East, the Greco-Roman World and Modern Astronomy", edited by van Kooten, Brill, Leiden
von Stuckrad, Kocku (2015), "Stars and Powers: Astrological Thinking in Imperial Politics from the Hasmoneans to Bar Kokhba", in "The Star of Bethlehem and the Magi", see van Kooten!
White, Gavin (2014), "Babylonian Star-lore – An Illustrated Guide to the Star-lore and Constellations of Ancient Babylonia", Solaria Publications, London
Vitruvius Pollio, Marcus, "De Architectura", written in the first century BC or AD
Zaehner, Robert Charles (1961), "The Dawn and Twilight of Zoroastrianism", G. P. Putnam's sons, New York

Registry

Aaron Adair. *See* Adair
Actium, 153
Adair, 85, 98
Adversus Haereses. See Against Heresies
Against Heresies, 80
Akkad, 32, 38, 65
Akkadian Empire, 65
Alexander the Great, 53, 56, 67, 68, 102
Amorite, 38
Amurru, 38, 39, 93, 114, 180
Antigonus, 150, 151, 156
Antipater, 156, 162
Antony. *See* Mark Antony
Anu, 73
Apelleus (Macedonian month), 142
Arabic Infancy Gospel, 62
Archangel Michael, 52, 73
Archelaus, 70, 129, 137, 158, 159, 165
Archer, 24
Asclepius, 73
Asfar Malwasia. *See* Sfar Malwasia

Ashur, 75
Ashurbanipal, 33
Assur. *See Assyria*
Assyria, 65, 75
Assyrian kingdom. *See Assyria*
asterism, 13
astrology, 29
Augustine, 83
Augustus, 58, 70, 153, 154, 158, 162, 167
Avesta, 124
Babylon, 68, 74
Babylonian captivity, 66
Babylonian kingdom. *See Old or New Babylonian Kingdom*
Balaam, 44, 60
Bar Kokhba, 45
Berossos, 41, 72, 110
Biltcliffe, 144
Book of Enoch, 50
Brundisium, 146
Bull, 121
Caesarea, 155
Caius Asinius Pollio, 146
Caius Domitius Calvinus, 146
calendar, 35, 148
Calgary, 197
Caligula, 161

Caninius Gallus, 148
Cassius Dio, 152
Centaur. *See* Archer
Chaldean, 56, 59, 159
Chaldei. *See* Chaldean
Chasleu (Jewish month), 142
Claudius, 139
Cleopatra, 69, 146
comet, 88
conjunction, 23
constellation, 89
consul, 146, 148
consuls, year of, 135
Cor Leonis. *See* Regulus
crown, 18
Ctesias of Cnidus, 144
cubit, 37
cuneiform, 34
cuneiform script, 72
Cyrus II of Persia. *See* Cyrus the Great
Cyrus the Great, 66
Darius III, 67
degree, 37
Derech Beit Lechem, 97
Devil, 171
diary, 35
divination, 29, 54

dragon, 109
Ea. *See* Enki
eagle, 73, 76
ecliptic, 19, 36
Egypt, 41, 64, 67
Egyptian system, 134, 153
Elam, 39
Enki, 73
Enlil, 73
Enuma Anu Enlil, 7, 32, 33, 35, 38
Enuma Elish, 74
Epiphanius, 82
Eridu, 73
Esagila, 33
Essenes, 50, 159
ethnarch, 70
Eusebius, 136, 140
exaltation, 115
Ezekiel, 76
fall of Jerusalem, 137
Fiery Trine, 24
finger (measurement), 37
flood, 72, 122
Gabinius, 143
Galilee, 70
Gaugamela, 67
Geographica, 143
Gilgamesh, 72
gnostic, 80
Golgatha. *See* Calgary
gospel, 76
gospel, symbols of, 76
great conjunction, 24, 89
Greek calendar. *See* Calendar
Halley's Comet, 88
Hammurabi, 65, 74

Hegedus, 10, 18
Hercules, 110
Herod, 70, 129, 146, 151, 156, 160, 164, 167
Herod Antipas, 70, 161, 163
Herod Archelaus. *See* Archelaus
Herod Philip. *See* Philip
Herod the Great. *See* Herod
Herodotus, 53
hidden place. *See* Secret place
Hipparchus, 18
horn, of the moon, 35
Hutchinson, 103, 108, 129
Hydra, 52, 73, 110, 112
inclusive counting, 154
Irenaeus of Lyon, 60, 80, 173
Ishtar, 34, 74
Israel, 69
Jerome, 82
Jerusalem, 148
John, 80
John the Evangelist, 170
John the Presbyter, 78, 108, 170
Josephus, 131, 141, 155, 168
Judah, 69
Judea (Latin). *See* Judah
Jupiter, 26, 34, 74, 91
Justin Martyr, 60
Kassite, 65

King of Akkad, 32
King of Kish, 64
Kish, 64
Kokhba, 45
Kooten. *See* van Kooten
Kos, 41, 72
Lamashtu, 120
Larson, 94, 96
latitude, 17
Learnian Hydra. *See* Hydra
Leo. *See* Lion
Libya, 67
Lion, 13, 16, 24, 34, 74, 76, 91
Livy, 136, 137
longitude, 17
Lugal, 28
Luke, 178
LXX. *See* Septuagint
Macedonia, 67
Macedonian system, 134, 153
magi, 1, 53, 54, 58, 59, 96
magi, as sorcerer, 58
magi, as wise men, 62
magician, 53
magus (singular). *See* magi (plural)
Mandaeism, 42
Manichaeism, 43
Marcus Agrippa, 148
Marduk, 33, 41, 72, 74
Mark Antony, 146, 150, 153
Mars, 26, 34, 74
Mary, 43
Mercury, 27, 34, 52, 75, 110
Mesopotamia, 63

204

meteor, 87
Michael, 111
Moon, 35
Moses, 61
MUL, 34
Mul Apin, 31
Mushmahhu, 110
Nabopolassar, 66
Nabu, 34, 74, 75
natal chart, 29
Nebuchadnezzar, 66, 75
Neo-Assyrian empire. *See* Assyria
Nergal, 34, 74
Nero, 57
New Year, 134
Nicolaus of Damascus, 137, 141, 143, 144, 164
Ninhursag, 34, 73
Ninurta, 34, 73, 75, 110, 121
normal star, 36
novae, 88
Numbers, 44, 60
occult, 90
Old Babylonian Kingdom, 65
Olympiad, 140, 143
omen, 32
omens, compare, 185
Origin, 61
Parthia, 53, 69
Parthian, 152
Path of the Moon, 20
Paul, 49
peace, 99, 117, 183
Perea, 70
Persepolis, 53, 67
Persia, 53, 66

Pheroras, 162
Philip II, 67
Philip the Tetrarch, 158
Pisces, 90
planet, 13, 34
planet, stationary. *See* stationary point
Platonic philosophy, 172
Polybius, 142
Polykarpus, 80, 83
Pompey, 150
Pontus Pilate, 70, 160
precession, 18
pregnancy, 107
prograde, 22
Ptolemy, 67
Quintus Curtius Rufus. *See* Rufus
Quintus Hortensius, 141
Quintus Metellus, 141
Quirinius, 127, 129
Qumran, 50
Rabmag, 54
Ram, 24
regnal year, 133, 139, 140, 152
Regulus, 27, 91
retrograde, 21, 22
Revelation, 180
Rome, 68
Rufus, 56
Sagittarius. *See* Archer
Sargon of Akkad, 65
Saturn, 26, 34, 73, 121
secret place, 115, 180
Seleucia, 68

Seleucus, 67, 68
Semitic, 64
Septuagint, 178
seven headed dragon, 73, 109
Sfar Malvasia, 42
shepherds, 179
Sirius, 36
Sivan, 148
Smyrna, 80
sorcerer, 58
St George, 73
St Irenaeus. *See* Ireneaus of Lyon
stationary point, 22, 36
Strabo, 137, 143, 144, 150, 164
Subartu, 39
Sumerians, 64
supernovae, 88
Syria, 66
Taurus, 34, 76
taxation, 127
tetrarch, 158, 162
The Antiquities of the Jews, 136
The Fishes. *See* Pisces
The Jewish War, 136
The Strange Star, 23
Tiberius, 139, 158, 160
trine, 24, 90
Utu, 74
van Kooten, 55, 57, 59
Varus, 165
watch, 35
vates. *See* diviner
Venus, 27, 34, 74
Venus, dimmed, 107
Virgin, 34, 73, 121
Virgo. *See* Virgin

wise men. *See* magi
Vitellius, 160
Zoroaster, 62, 125
Zoroastrianism, 62, 124
Zurvanism, 126

Printed in Great Britain
by Amazon